John Foster

Oxford University Press

Oxford University Press, Walton Street, Oxford OX2 6DP

*Oxford New York Toronto*
*Delhi Bombay Calcutta Madras Karachi*
*Petaling Jaya Singapore Hong Kong Tokyo*
*Nairobi Dar es Salaam Cape Town*
*Melbourne Auckland*

and associated companies in
*Berlin Ibadan*

*Oxford* is a trade mark of Oxford University Press

© Selection and notes: John Foster 1991

Second impression 1992

ISBN 0 19 831264 4

All rights reserved. This publication may not be reproduced, stored or transmitted, in any forms or by any means, except in accordance with the terms of licenses issued by the Copyright Licensing Agency, or except for fair dealing for the purposes of research or private study, or criticism or review, as permitted under the Copyright, Designs and Patents Act, 1988. Enquiries concerning reproduction outside those terms should be addressed to the Permissions Department, Oxford University Press.

The cover illustration is by Mark Dobson

Typeset by Pentacor PLC, High Wycombe, Bucks
Printed in Great Britain

# Contents

| | |
|---|---|
| Acknowledgements | v |
| Preface | vii |

## *Football Crazy* — 1

| | |
|---|---|
| The Trial  *Tony Drake* | 1 |
| The Commentator  *Gareth Owen* | 6 |
| A Soccer Star Narrowly Missed  *Joseph D. Knight* | 9 |
| World Cup  *Paul Higgins* | 10 |
| Unfair  *Michael Rosen* | 11 |
| Dad  *Joanna White* | 12 |
| The Big Match  *Barry Hines* | 13 |
| Clakker May  *Michael Parkinson* | 18 |
| I Didn't Do Nothing  *Brian Glanville* | 23 |
| The Ref's a Woman!  *Paul Wilson* | 28 |

## *Sports at School* — 30

| | |
|---|---|
| The Screams of the Damned  *Adèle Geras* | 30 |
| That Showed 'Em  *Roger Mills* | 32 |
| Skivers  *David Williams* | 35 |
| After Sports Day  *John Foster* | 46 |
| Aliens  *Brain Keaney* | 47 |
| Feet  *Jan Mark* | 55 |
| Games Should Not be Compulsory  *Dorian Wood* | 64 |
| Miss Willis PE  *Judith Nicholls* | 66 |
| Caught in the Act  *Lesley Davies* | 68 |

## *Practice Makes Perfect* — 69

| | |
|---|---|
| High Dive  *James Kirkup* | 69 |
| Practice Makes Perfect  *Daley Thompson* | 70 |
| A Life in the Day of Joanne Conway  *Jenny Woolf* | 73 |
| Lean Lesson  *Matthew Bridgeman* | 77 |
| Boxer Man In-a Skippin' Workout  *James Berry* | 79 |

Contents

## *Track and Field* — 80

| | |
|---|---|
| To James  *Frank Horne* | 80 |
| Raymond's Run  *Toni Cade Bambara* | 81 |
| Hero  *Mick Gowar* | 87 |
| The High Jump Competition  *Peter Carter* | 89 |
| A Girl Called Golden  *David Bateson* | 114 |
| The Eighth Paralympic Games, Seoul 1988  *Bill Boyle* | 116 |

## *But Is It Sport?* — 118

| | |
|---|---|
| Pop's Boy  *Irvin Ashkenazy* | 118 |
| Who Killed Davey Moore?  *Bob Dylan* | 123 |
| Glove me Tender  *Kolton Lee* | 125 |
| A-hunting I Will Go, Without Shame  *Kathleen Peyton* | 127 |
| Moral Rules to Every Game  *Sam Ramsamy* | 129 |
| The Progress of Sport  *Raymond Wilson* | 131 |

## *Sport on TV* — 133

| | |
|---|---|
| Points of View | 133 |
| The Dartist  *Alan Bold* | 137 |
| Sumo Wrestlers  *James Kirkup* | 138 |
| The Game's All About Clichés, innit?  *Fritz Spiegl* | 140 |

## *Just for Fun* — 142

| | |
|---|---|
| Playing for Wales  *Max Boyce* | 142 |
| The Village Cricket Match  *Ian McDonald* | 144 |
| The Day I Ran for England  *Geraldine Kaye* | 148 |

## Activities — 152

## Extended Activities — 179

## Wider Reading — 181

# Acknowledgements

The editor and publisher are grateful for permission to use the following copyright materials.

**Irvin Ashkenazy**: 'Pop's Boy' from *Sports Stories*, WLE Short Stories 3, pp. 76–80. Reprinted by permission of Ward Lock Educational Co. Ltd. **Toni Cade Bambara**: 'Raymond's Run' from *Gorilla My Love*. Reprinted by permission of The Women's Press Ltd. **David Bateson**: 'A Girl Called Golden' © 1991 David Bateson. Reprinted by permission of the author. **James Berry**: 'Boxer Man In-a Skippin Workout' from *When I Dance*. Reprinted by permission of Hamish Hamilton. **Alan Bold**: 'The Dartist', © 1991 Alan Bold. Reprinted by permission of the author. **Max Boyce**: 'Playing for Wales' reprinted from *I Was There* (Weidenfeld & Nicholson Ltd). Copyright Max Boyce. **Bill Boyle**: 'The Eighth Paralympic Games, Seoul 1988', © 1991 Bill Boyle. Reprinted by permission of the author. **Matthew Bridgeman**: 'Lean Lesson' from *Today's Runner*, September 1988. Copyright Today's Runner Magazine 1988. Reprinted with permission. **Peter Carter**: 'The High Jump Competition' from *Bury the Dead*, pp. 254–277. Reprinted by permission of Oxford University Press. **Lesley Davies**: 'Caught in the Act'. Reprinted by permission of the author. **Tony Drake: 'The Trial'** © 1991 Tony Drake. Reprinted by permission of the author. **Bob Dylan**: 'Who Killed Davey Moore?'. © Warner Chappell Music Ltd. Reproduced by permission of Warner Chappell Music Ltd. *John Foster*: 'After Sports Day', © 1991 John Foster. Reprinted by permission of the author. **Adèle Geras**: from *Other Echoes*, © Adèle Geras 1982. Reprinted by permission of Laura Cecil, Literary Agent on behalf of Adèle Geras. **Brian Glanville**: 'I didn't do nothing' extracted from *Goalkeepers are Crazy*. Copyright Brian Glanville, reproduced by permission of John Farquharson Ltd, London. **Paul Higgins**: 'World Cup' from *Madtail, Miniwhale and Other Shape Poems*, ed. Wes Magee (Kestrel Books). Copyright Paul Higgins. **Barry Hines**: 'The Big Match'. Reprinted by permission of the author. **Frank Horne**: 'To James' from *Contemporary English* 1, ed. John Foster (Macmillan, London Ltd). **Geraldine Kaye**: 'The Day I Ran for England', © 1991 Geraldine Kaye. Reprinted by permission of the author. **Brian Keaney**: 'Aliens' from *Don't Hang About*, pp. 56–66. Reprinted by permission of Oxford University Press. **James Kirkup**: 'High Dive', © 1991 James Kirkup, and 'Sumo

# Acknowledgements

Wrestlers' from *Paper Windows: Poems from Japan* (Dent). Both reprinted by permission of the author. **Joseph D Knight**: 'A Soccer Star Narrowly Missed' from *There Was a Young Fellow Called Glover*, ed. Simon Barnes (Kingswood Press). Reprinted with permission. **Kolton Lee**: 'Glove me tender', from *Raging Belles*, *Sky Magazine*, September 1988. Reproduced by permission of *Sky Magazine*/Katz. **Ian McDonald**: 'The village cricket match', adapted from *The Humming-Bird Tree* (Heinemann). **Jan Mark**: 'Feet' from *Feet and Other Stories* (Kestrel Books, 1983), © 1980 Jan Mark. Reprinted by permission of Penguin Books Ltd. **Roger Mills**: 'That showed 'em' taken from *A Comprehensive Education*. Reprinted by permission of Centerprise Publications. **Judith Nicholls**: 'Miss Willis, P.E.', © 1991 Judith Nicholls. Reprinted by permission of the author. **Gareth Owen**: 'The Commentator' from *Song of the City*. *Reprinted by permission of Collins Publishers. **K. M. Peyton**: 'A-hunting I will go, without shame'. © 1981 K. M. Peyton. First published in *The Guardian*. Reprinted by permission of the author. **Michael Parkinson**: 'Clakker May' from *Football Daft* (Stanley Paul Publ). Reprinted with permission. Extracts from *Points of View* by Barry Took reproduced with the permission of BBC Enterprises Ltd. **Sam Ramsamy**: 'Moral rules to every game', first published in *The Independent*, 12 August 1989. Reprinted with permission. **Michael Rosen**: 'Unfair' from *Quick Let's Get Out of Here*. Reprinted by permission of Andre Deutsch Ltd. **Fritz Spiegl**: 'The game's all about clichés, innit?', first published in *The Independent*, 1 September 1988. © 1988 Fritz Spiegl. **Daley Thompson**: 'Practice makes perfect' reprinted from *One Is My Lucky Number*. Reprinted by permission of W H Allen plc. **Joanna White**: 'Dad', © 1991 Joanna White. Reprinted with permission. **David Williams**: 'Skivers', © 1991 David Williams. Reprinted by permission of the author. **Paul Wilson**: 'Paying the price of pride and prejudice', first published in *The Independent*, 10 February 1990. Reprinted with permission. **Raymond Wilson**: 'The progress of sport', © 1991 Raymond Wilson. Reprinted by permission of the author. **Dorian Wood**: 'Games should not be compulsory', *Teachers' Weekly*, 10 October 1988. Reprinted with permission. **Jenny Woolf**: 'A Life in the Day of Joanne Conway', *The Sunday Times*, 15 January 1989. © Times Newspapers Ltd 1989. Reprinted with permission.

Although every effort has been made to secure reprint permission prior to publication this has not always proved possible. If contacted the publisher with be pleased to rectify any errors or omissions at the earliest opportunity.

# Preface

*Sport* consists of a range of contemporary writing about sport. The aim is to present students with a wide variety of types of writing, in both fiction and non-fiction, that provide insights into the part that sport plays in our lives. Thus, in addition to stories and poems, there are magazine and newspaper articles, autobiographical accounts and a short play, which was specially written for this collection.

The book is divided into seven sections, each of which focuses on a different aspect of sport. The pieces in *Football Crazy* and *Track and Field* deal with the experiences of footballers and athletes, and raise issues connected with these sports, such as football violence, the opportunities for women to play football and the taking of drugs to enhance performances. *Sports at School* reflects the experiences of those who dislike games, as well as of those who enjoy them, and contains an article questioning whether games should be a compulsory part of the curriculum. *Practice makes Perfect* includes articles which reveal the dedication and single-mindedness of athletes ambitious for success, while among the articles in *Just for Fun* there is Max Boyce's light-hearted memories of childhood games, an account of an unusual cricket match and Geraldine Kaye's wry reflections on her career as an athlete. *Sport on TV* includes a series of letters expressing viewers' opinions of TV sports coverage and an article on the clichés often used by sports commentators. In *But is it Sport?* the focus in on boxing and hunting and there is also an article on the question of whether sport can ever be neutral in political or moral terms.

A final section provides background information about the source of each piece, about the writers and give ideas for follow-up work. These suggestions have deliberately been kept separate

## Preface

from the main body of the text, so that the pieces can be read in the way a student or a teacher wishes, and the follow-up work developed as appropriate to individuals and groups.

In addition to activities, discussion work and written assignments on the individual pieces in the anthology, the final section includes a number of suggestions for extended assignments and for wider reading. It is hoped that reading the pieces in this anthology will not only be a pleasurable experience for students and provoke a thoughtful response, but that it will also stimulate them to read more widely and to explore further the issues that are raised.

*John Foster*

# *Football Crazy*
# The Trial

*Tony Drake*

On the morning of the trial match, I had one of those weird experiences where I came up out of a deep sleep and, for a split second, I couldn't think who I was or where I was. It's really frightening when it happens, like you're all alone and totally lost in an empty world, but it soon passes. I rolled out of bed and the first thing I saw was my kit bag already packed from the night before. I wanted to make a quick exit, see, before anyone started asking awkward questions.

I would have got away with it too, if my sister Marcia hadn't come stumbling into the kitchen just as I was heading out of the back door.

'Where you off to?' she asked, rubbing the sleep from her eyes. 'We don't expect to see you this early on a Saturday morning.'

'I got a football match,' I mumbled, stepping out into the back yard. 'See you.'

But Marcia wasn't put off that easy. She followed me out of the back door, clutching her bath robe round her.

'Football?' she said. 'But you don't play football on Saturday. You only play Sundays.'

'Not this week,' I told her. 'I got a game this morning. All right?'

She'd know soon enough. A couple of hours and it'd all be over. Then I'd be able to tell her, my parents, Jan and anyone else who wanted to know. And that'd be an end to it all. Right?

Skelcher was already in the changing rooms when I got down there, scribbling on his clipboard. The kit was laid out on the benches in neat little piles, shirts, shorts and socks. As soon as I saw it, it all came back to me. That feeling of anticipation, a sort of nervous excitement, you know, just like the first time I'd ever got picked for a proper game back at Jubilee Street, the first time I ever got to go out on a real pitch for a team where we all wore the same colour shirts.

'Number ten, Colin,' Skelcher said. 'Number ten in the red, OK? You'll be up against Oggy like you wanted.'

'Oggy?' I said.

'That centre back,' Skelcher reminded me, 'from the last trial match.'

*Oggy*. That figured. He looked like an Oggy, and when we got out on the field, he played like an Oggy. Every high cross that got hit into the box, he'd give this loud bellow – 'Oggy's!' – and thump the ball back up the field with his boot or his head. It didn't matter which; it went just as far either way.

And he had a whole gang of his mates on the touch-line, who kept up a running commentary on everything he did.

'Played, Oggy!' they'd shout every time he went for the ball. 'Give it some, Oggy.'

He could tackle too. Every time I got a sniff of the ball in the early part of the game, he was right up my back, kicking like a mule in boots. And every time he kicked me up in the air, I'd hear the same thing from the touch-line.

'Show him, Oggy!'

And me? I was getting nowhere. This was nothing like the Sunday morning football I'd got used to, where most of the players were running off the skinful they'd had the night before. With them you got a bit of time to stop on the ball and take a look round, but not in this game. If it wasn't Oggy kicking me up in the air, there'd be two or three more snapping at my ankles. I couldn't get going at all.

It got so bad that the other players in my team stopped passing the ball to me. And every time I looked across at Skelcher on the touch-line, he was hiding behind his clipboard. If he was feeling embarrassed about inviting me for a trial, that was nothing to

# The Trial

what I was feeling out on the pitch. All I could do was run up and down the field, calling for passes that never came.

'It's even easier than last time,' I heard Oggy call to his mates when the ball went out for a throw in on their side of the pitch. 'I don't know where Skelcher digs them up from.'

What made me really mad was that he was right. For two weeks I'd kept this trial all to myself, telling no one about it, just so I could come out and show Oggy and all the rest how football should be played. But now that the time had come, I couldn't do anything right. As far as the people on the line were concerned, I was just another kid with ideas too big for him.

*I didn't ask to be here* – I felt like screaming at them – *it was him who asked me to play.*

'Relax,' Skelcher told me at half time. 'You're trying too hard.'

But I knew he didn't really mean it. And I knew that if I didn't do something soon, he'd have me off and give my shirt to one of the subs who were jumping up and down on the touch-line just itching to get on the field.

The second half got under way and I still couldn't get going. I could see Skelcher warming up a couple of subs and I knew my time was running out fast, but what could I do? If no one passed me the ball, how could I show them what I was capable of?

Then, out of the blue, a loose ball came my way. *Now* – I thought – *this time I'll show them!* I lifted my head to take a quick look and, as I did so, Oggy hit me from behind like a runaway train.

'Again, Oggy!' came the chorus from the touch-line. 'Show him who's boss.'

This time, though, the ref had blown up for the foul and we had a free kick about thirty yards from goal. Oggy wasted no time pulling players back into a five man wall, and I stood on the ball with our captain, a red haired midfield player called Bren. Skelcher had made him captain because he was already on United's books as an apprentice.

'You got any ideas?' he asked me.

I shrugged.

3

*Football Crazy*

'Tell you what then,' he suggested. 'You step over the ball and I'll try to curl it round the wall.'

I nodded. It made sense. Just the sort of move I liked to see myself when it came off: a touch of real class. Yeah, it made sense all right.

But as I ran towards the ball, I caught a glimpse of Oggy's face sneering at me from the wall, and something flipped in my mind. I didn't step over the ball like Bren had told me to. Instead I hit it with every bit of strength I had and sent it screaming straight at Oggy's head.

He wasn't expecting that any more than Bren was. His mouth fell open and he tried to jerk his head out of the way. He almost managed it too, but the ball caught him on the ear and ricocheted into the net with the goalkeeper going the wrong way.

For a moment or two, no one said a word. I turned away like I always do, with one arm in the air, and caught sight of the puzzled look on Bren's face. Then he started laughing.

'All right,' he grinned. 'Do it your own way.'

From then on, I did. That one shot, see, it made all the difference, especially the way it went in off Oggy's ear. Perfect that was, and I knew I could do him now. First chance I got, from a through pass, I took it down in one, dragged it left with the outside of my boot and then swayed away to the right. I nearly wet myself to see Oggy come tanking in, missing me *and* the ball. I finished off that move with a cross to the far post that Bren headed into the net.

'Like I said,' he grinned when he came over to slap hands, 'we'll do it your way.'

And that wasn't the last time I left Oggy on his backside. Time and again I had him beat, and his mates on the touch-line didn't have anything to shout about any more. It was open house for us now. We were all going past him whenever we wanted.

Five minutes from time, I ran at him in the box, took him left, took him right, and then shoved the ball right through his legs. Nutmeg! I wanted to laugh out loud then, but Oggy was so angry he grabbed me round the waist when I went past him and brought me down with a rugby tackle.

'You clever bastard!' he spat in my ear as he climbed up off me.

'Yeah,' I hissed back, 'too clever for you, eh?'

I think he might have hit me if the ref hadn't been right on the spot, blowing up for the penalty. Bren let me take the kick and I beat the keeper easily with a kick that would have ended up in the river if the net hadn't been there to catch it.

I knew then why I'd decided to play in this trial match. It wasn't for Skelcher or Oggy or anyone else. It was for me. It was for that feeling I got when I first pulled on the shirt, or when I buried that penalty kick in the back of the net. Feelings like that, you can pretend to live without them, but you never forget them, not completely.

'See?' Skelcher said when the game was over. 'I told you it'd all come back to you if you'd only relax.'

'So what happens now?' I asked him.

He winked and tapped the side of his nose.

'Leave it with me, Colin,' he whispered. 'Just you leave it with me.'

*Football Crazy*

# The Commentator

*Gareth Owen*


Good afternoon and welcome,
This is Danny Markey your commentator
Welcoming you to this international
Between England and Holland,
Which is being played here this afternoon
At four Florence Terrace.
And the pitch looks in superb condition
As Danny Markey prepares
To kick off for England;
And this capacity crowd roars
As Markey, the England captain,
Puts England on the attack.
Straight away it's Markey
With a lovely pass to Keegan,
Keegan back to Markey,
Markey in possession now
Jinking skilfully past the dustbin
And a neat flick inside the cat there,
What a brilliant player this Markey is
And still only nine years old!
Markey to Francis
Francis to Markey,
Markey is through . . .
No, he's been tackled by the drainpipe;
But he's won the ball back brilliantly
And he's advancing on the Dutch keeper now,
It must be a goal
He comes off his line
But Markey chips him brilliantly

## The Commentator

It's a goal . . .
No.
It's gone into Mrs Spence's next door.
And Markey's going round
To ask for his ball back.
The Crowd is silent now
If he can't get the ball back
It could be the end of this international.
And now the door's opening
And yes, it's Mrs Spence,
Mrs Spence has come to the door,
And wait a minute, she's shaking her head,
She is shaking her head,
She is not going to let Markey
Have his ball back.
What is the referee going to do?
Markey looks very dejected here,
He's walking back, hanging his head . . .
What's he doing now?
He seems to be waiting
And my goodness me
He's going back,
Markey is going back for the ball,
What a brilliant and exciting move;
He waited until the front door was closed
And then went back for that lost ball.
He's searching now,
He's searching for that ball
Down there by the compost heap
And wait a minute
He's found it!
He's found that ball
And that's marvellous news
For the hundred thousand fans gathered here,
Who are showing their appreciation
In no uncertain fashion.

*Football Crazy*

But wait a minute,
The door's opening once more;
It's her, it's Mrs Spence!
And she's waving her fist
And shouting something
But I can't make out what it is.
She's obviously not pleased.
And Markey's off,
He's running round in circles
Dodging this way and that
With Mrs Spence in hot pursuit,
And he's past her,
What skills this boy has.
But Mr Spence is here too
And Bruce their dog,
Markey is going to have to
Pull out something extra
To get out of this one;
He's only got Mr Spence and the bassett
To beat now. He's running straight at him.
And he's down, he's down on all fours;
What is he doing?
And Oh my goodness
That is brilliant,
That is absolutely brilliant,
He's gone between Spence's legs.
But he's got him,
This rugged tackler has got him,
He's got him by the jacket,
And Bruce is in there too,
Bruce has him by the seat of the pants,
He'll never get out of this one.
But he has,
He has got away;
He wriggled out of his jacket
And left part of his trousers with Bruce;

This boy is absolute dynamite.
He's over the wall, he's clear,
They'll never catch him now,
He's on his bike and
Through the front gate
And I don't think we'll see any more of Markey
Till the coast's clear
And it's safe to come home;
So this is Danny Markey . . .
Handing you back to the studio.

# A Soccer Star Narrowly Missed

*Joseph D. Knight*

A soccer star narrowly missed
The goal, and was grieved to be hissed
    So he broke down in tears
    To ironic cheers
'Cos he'd hoped to be cuddled and kissed.

*Football Crazy*

# World Cup

*Paul Higgins*

# Unfair

*Michael Rosen*

When we went over the park
Sunday mornings
To play football
we picked up sides.

Lizzie was our striker
because she had the best shot.

When the teachers
chose the school team
Marshy was our striker.

Lizzie wasn't allowed to play,
they said

So she watched us lose, instead . . .

*Football Crazy*

# Dad

*Joanna White*

In memory of those who died at Hillsborough, April 1989

Is it Saturday yet, Dad?
Have you got the tickets, Dad?
Are we going by train, Dad?
Will it be a good game, Dad?
Is it far to walk now, Dad?
Can you buy me a scarf, Dad?
Aren't there lots of people, Dad?
Can we go down to the front, Dad?
I am so very crushed, Dad!
I can hardly see, Dad!
I can't breathe, Dad!
*Dad*! . . . . . Dad! . . . . . dad! . . .

# The Big Match

*Barry Hines*

I've never played a game of football in my life. I've always played in matches. I was brought up in an area dominated by professional football clubs – Barnsley, Sheffield, Rotherham, Doncaster, Huddersfield, Leeds. There were no prominent amateur clubs to watch, so my attitudes were formed on the terraces at Barnsley, Sheffield Wednesday and United.

There were hundreds of local football teams around, but these were never amateurs either. Not in spirit anyway. They were composed of lads who were aspiring to be professionals, or men who hadn't made it. The game was never the thing. Only the winning. The only good matches were the ones that you won. It was as simple as that.

At Grammar School they thought differently. They even wasted part of the field on a pitch which had funny markings and two flag poles stuck at each end. I still think there is something unsatisfactory about Rugby posts. There is no real end to them for a start. If you kick the ball five miles high and the referee judges that it would have gone between the posts then it's a goal. But even then it's not a *real* goal is it? Real goals are under the cross-bar. And they have nets. I can never get worked up when I see a rugby player taking a penalty kick, no matter how far the distance, or how narrow the angle. After all, he only has to kick the ball over the bar, and there's nobody trying to stop it at that. Footballers do this all the time and get jeered and cursed for it, even though they are running with the ball, or being tackled, or being blocked by a wall of players standing five yards away instead of ten. No, if there was a goalkeeper up there between the posts, suspended by balloons, or with a helicopter strapped to his back, then I might be able to take it more seriously.

13

I even find the markings on a football pitch satisfying; their symmetry, the matching halves of boxes and curves. It's as pleasing to the eye as the doubles in dominoes. I'm surprised no artist has painted a football pitch yet, just the white lines on a green background. Hanging in a gallery nothing else would get a look in. There'd be a crowd round it all day long just waiting for the teams to come out.

At Grammar School they tried to convince me that football was not really important, that games lessons were merely half-time breaks between the academic rigours of the week. But what they did not understand was that I was not an academic boy. All I wanted to be was a professional footballer. At school I lived from games lessons to Saturday morning matches, year in, year out. The agonies I've sat through staring out of the window hoping that the fog would clear, or the rain would stop, before the games lesson. The weeks that have been ruined when the teacher has said that the weather was too inclement and we would have to go into a classroom and have a quiz.

There's a Grammar School teacher's word for you, inclement. When we couldn't play at home it was because it was pissing it down.

We didn't play in leagues either. There were no cups and we couldn't play for the district team. That was only for the local secondary modern school boys. This used to infuriate and frustrate me, the way we were supposed to regard ourselves as above this kind of competition. Why did they want to make us feel superior? Just because I sat down one morning when I was ten years old and got a few more sums right than my mates seemed no reason for trying to make me into a snob. Yet this is what they tried to do. Not overtly, but the very existence of the school meant they had no choice. Like the Public School, the Grammar school exists to perpetuate the class divisions within our society. They are middle-class institutions which seduce the working-class student into their rank.

They failed with me. When my mates left secondary modern school at fifteen, I wanted to leave with them. I applied to the

# The Big Match

local pit for a job as an apprentice mining surveyor. I didn't want to be a surveyor, but it seemed a respectable sort of job; I would be on the staff. The chief surveyor said, you need 'O' levels for this job, go back to school and get some. So I went back and got some. And when I knew the rainfall on the Pampas and Gladstone's Foreign Policy, they employed me as an apprentice mining surveyor.

I stuck it for six months. At the time I was playing for Barnsley Juniors. The matches were on Saturday mornings. Unfortunately I was supposed to work Saturday mornings. So I had no choice. I had to give up my job.

I went back to school and decided to become a P.E. Teacher. I thought that if I didn't make it as a professional footballer, then teaching Physical Education would be the next best thing. Like football, I didn't regard it as work. I didn't want to be a teacher. To my mind they were on a par with the police, agents of repression. No, it just seemed like a very pleasant way of perpetuating my adolescence, that is all.

I think this is one of the reasons why I never made it though. I took out an insurance policy. I wanted something to fall back on. I was a decent player, but I would have been a lot better if the only alternatives had been the track at Fords' or working all three shifts down the pit like my dad.

It was while I was in the sixth form that something very significant happened to me. I was chosen to attend the Schools Week at Cambridge. About one hundred of the supposedly best Grammar school and Public school footballers were picked to take part in a series of trial matches, the aim being to find the best team to play Scotland under-eighteens.

I went down on that train from Sheffield full of myself. I was seventeen, fit, fast, strong and reasonably skilful. I was captain of the school team, I was playing for Yorkshire Grammar Schools and several league clubs were interested in me. A Manchester United Scout had been to our house, and this was at the time of the great team, just before the Munich Disaster.

I went down in my suit – I was a semi-Ted at the time – drape

*Football Crazy*

jacket, tight trousers, crew cut, D.A. When I saw those Public School boys I couldn't believe it. They didn't seem to have heard of fashion. They were all dressed in flannels and sports jackets, with sloping haircuts. They would have looked well in the officers' mess in a British war film. Nigel Patrick would have been their commanding officer.

But it was when we talked together that I really felt the difference. They were so articulate and so assured. They had a collective air of massive superiority that staggered me. And suddenly I didn't want to talk, I was embarrassed by my thick Barnsley accent. I was even embarrassed by my clothes; I was a northern herbert in yellow socks and bumpers. They tolerated me, after all they were too well bred to be rude, but all the time I felt I was being politely patronized.

Disraeli was wrong when he talked about two nations. It's more like two worlds.

The only place I could match them was on the football pitch. I didn't have to say very much there. Some of them were good players, but even the best lacked the urgency and determination of the working-class Grammar school boys. But then, what had they to be urgent about? Football was not important in their lives. For them it really was a game. They had more studied destinations. They were from wealthy influential families, they were destined for Oxford and Cambridge, and then into positions which would in turn ensure and perpetuate the wealth and influence of their own class. What was the tawdry glamour of football, compared to the stealthy power and affluence that they were going to achieve?

I began to realize that playing for Barnsley for £20 a week wasn't the real big-time after all. It was tin-pot, a mere diversion, compared to that other world that I was now getting a look at for the first time in my life.

I made the England team. I watched every match I did not play in to assess all the other midfield players on the course. There was only one danger for my position, a boy from a public school. But he got injured. I was glad. He was no better than me,

## The Big Match

but he might have been picked because he looked more respectable, and he would certainly have known how to speak to the waiters in the hotel in Glasgow.

We played Scotland at Celtic Park. I can't remember much about the match except the score; we lost 0–3. It didn't seem all that important though. What had been much more valuable was the political experience, seeing the class system at work close-up. For the first time I had been able to place football into some kind of social perspective.

For the real winners, of course, are those who play it as a game. Me? I'm still trying to get a team together, and keeping in training for the big match.

# Clakker May

*Michael Parkinson*

Goalkeepers like things that go bump in the night, defy analysis. They are as much a mystery in the general order of things as the function of the human appendix. It is, of course, relatively easy to explain what they have to do: their purpose is to prevent the ball entering the net by any means at their disposal, namely by catching it, punching it, kicking it, heading it out, or if they desire, throwing their caps at it. The mystery lies in the fact that this seemingly simple, straightforward task produces people of incredibly complex and often eccentric personality. Even today, when the game appears to be played by robots, when individuality is ruthlessly stifled at birth, the goalkeeper has survived with all his personal idiosyncracies intact. No one knows better than goalkeepers themselves that the price they pay for their freedom is to be talked about behind their backs. In the totalitarian regime of modern-day soccer they are treated as necessary screwballs. Because of this it is a commonly held belief that all goalkeepers have a slate loose, that the nature of the job being what it is, a man must be barmy to do it. The other theory is that the goalkeeper, because he is custodian of the most important part of a football field, slowly develops into a paranoiac.

I suspect that Clakker May would be regarded as a classic example by those people who reckon all goalkeepers are born crazy. You'd never suspect there was anything wrong by looking at him. He was a tall, stringy, quiet youth who lived with his parents and ten brothers and sisters in a council house near the pit gates. He became our goalkeeper quite by chance. One day we were a man short, and Len, our trainer, asked Clakker to play in goal. The result was a revelation. It wasn't so much when he donned the jersey he changed in his attitude towards his teammates, it was simply that he believed that the rules of the game related to everyone except himself.

We became aware of his quirk the first time he touched the ball. He left his goal line to meet a hard, high cross, caught the ball cleanly, shaped to clear downfield, and then, for no apparent reason, spun round and fled to the back of the net. This move dumbfounded players, officials and spectators alike. As we stood gaping, Clakker ran from the back of the net and booted the ball over the halfway line. Nobody moved as it bounced aimlessly towards the opposite goal and then the referee broke the silence by blowing on his whistle and pointing to the centre spot. This appeared to upset Clakker.

'What's tha' playin' at?' he asked the referee.

'I was just about to ask thee same question,' said the referee. By this time Len had run on to the field.

'What the bl.... hell . . . ' he began.

'Nay, Len. Tha' see I caught this ball and then I looks up and I saw this big centre forrard coming at me and I thought, "B.....r this lot", so I got out of his way,' Clakker explained.

'Tha' ran into t'bl.... net wi' t'ball and tha' scoored,' Len shouted.

'Scoored,' said Clakker, incredulously.

'Scoored,' said Len, emphatically.

Clakker shook his head. Len tried to keep calm. 'Look, lad,' he said, putting his arm round Clakker's shoulders. 'I know it's thi' first game and all that, but tha' must get one thing straight. When tha' catches t'ball gi' it some clog donwfield. Whatever tha' does don't run into t'net.'

Clakker nodded.

But it made little difference. In the next twenty minutes Clakker ran into the net thirteen times and we were losing 14–2. At this point the referee intervened. He called us all together and said: 'Na' look, lads, this is making a mock of a great game. If it goes on like this t'scoor will be in t'hundreds and I'll have to mek a report to t'League Management Committee and there'll

*Football Crazy*

be hell to pay.' We all nodded in agreement. The referee thought a bit and then said: 'What we'll do is amend t'rules. If Clakker runs into t'back of t'net in future it won't count as a goal, allus providin' he caught t'ball on t'right side of t'line in t'first place.'

Everyone agreed and play continued with this extraordinary amendment to the rules. At the final whistle we had lost fifteen to five and Clakker had shown that apart from his eccentric interpretation of the rules he was a remarkably good goalkeeper. Nobody said much after the game. It seemed useless to ask Clakker what went wrong because all of us agreed that like all goalkeepers he was a bit screwy. Our theory was confirmed by Clakker's old man, who when told of his son's extraordinary behaviour simply shook his head and said, 'He allus was a bit potty.'

But that was not the end of Clakker's career, not quite. He was picked for the next game because we didn't want to hurt him too much. Len, the trainer, called us together on the night before the game and explained how we might curb Clakker's madness. His plan was that the defenders should close in behind Clakker whenever he went out for a ball and bar his way into the net. Any resistance from Clakker should be firmly dealt with and if possible the ball taken from him and cleared upfield. In case Clakker should break through his own rearguard Len had taken the precaution of hiding the nets. His theory was that provided Clakker ran into goal, but straight out again, the referee would be unable to decide what had happened.

The reports of our last game had attracted a large crowd to the ground for Clakker's second appearance. All his family were present to see if it was true what people were saying about Clakker's extraordinary behaviour.

Things worked quite well for a time. Every time Clakker caught the ball we fell in around him and urged him away from his goal. Once he escaped us and nipped into goal, but he had the sense to escape immediately around the goalpost and clear downfield. The referee looked puzzled for a minute and gave

Clakker a peculiar look, but did not give a goal because he could not believe what he thought he saw. We were leading two goals to nil with five minutes of the first half left when Clakker gave the game away. Overconfident at having duped the referee once before, he ran over his own goal line with the ball. His plan came to grief when he collided with the iron stanchion at the back of the goal. As he staggered drunkenly against the support the referee blew for a goal and gave Clakker the sort of look that meant all was now revealed.

When half-time came none of us could look forward to the next forty-five minutes with any optimism. Len came on the field and beckoned myself and the centre half to one side. 'Na' look, lads, we've got to do something about yon Clakker,' he said. 'I've thought about playing him out of goal, but that's too dangerous. I can't just take him off because yon referee wouldn't allow it. So there's only one thing we can do.' He paused and looked at both of us.

'What's that?' I asked.

'Fix him,' said Len.

'Fix him?' I said.

Len nodded. 'When you get a chance, and as soon as you can, clobber him. I don't want him to get up, either,' said Len.

The centre half was smiling.

'Look,' I said to him, 'we can't clobber our own team-mate. It's not done.'

He looked at me pityingly. 'Leave it to me,' he said. 'I've fixed nicer people than Clakker.'

It took two minutes of the second half for Clakker to get fixed. There was a scrimmage in our goalmouth and when the dust had cleared Clakker lay prostrate on his goal line. Len came running on to the field, trying to look concerned. The centre half was trying hard to look innocent. Clakker's father had drifted over to the scene and was looking down at his son's body. 'He's better like that,' he said.

Len said to him, 'Tek your Clakker home and don't let him out till t'game's finished.'

*Football Crazy*

Clakker's old man nodded and signalled to some of his sons to pick Clakker up. The last we saw of them they were carrying Clakker out of the field and home. We did quite well without him and managed to win. Afterwards in the dressing room some of the lads were wondering how Clakker became injured. Len said: 'Tha' nivver can tell wi' goalkeepers. It's quite likely he laid himself out.'

# I Didn't Do Nothing

*Brian Glanville*

There's only one way to be a good referee. One way. Show 'em you'll stand no nonsense. As soon as a player thinks he can take liberties and get away with it, that's the end. Your authority's gone, and you might as well go home. Referees make me laugh when they say that this player always gives them trouble, or they don't like refereeing in this country or that one. As far as I'm concerned, one player's the same as another, and one *country's* the same as another.

I've refereed all over the world: Rome, Berlin, Rio, Paris, and I've never had any real trouble. That time in Montevideo, that was nothing, really; it was just blown up by the Press. All those stories about me being hit on the head with a bottle; it just brushed my shoulder, that was all, and as for being smuggled away afterwards in a car, it was the same car I came in.

There may have been one or two stones thrown, but they none of them hit *me*, I can tell you that. Authority, that's all you need, whether it's a British player or a Continental. With foreigners, especially the South Americans, you've got to be a bit firmer, that's all, it's Latin temperament. They come and they throw their arms about and they kiss each other when they score, but in the end it all comes down to the same thing. If they see you're the boss, they'll behave themselves.

There was a match in Santiago. I sent a player off and he wouldn't go. All right, I said, if you won't go, *I'll* go, and I walked off the field and abandoned the match. I'd like you to have seen their faces.

English footballers on the whole don't give you much bother; just the one or two, and we all know who *they* are; you soon learn to look out for them. Mind you, to tell the truth, I've found most of them easy enough. Other referees are always saying to me,

## Football Crazy

'Look out for so-and-so,' or 'You'd better be careful of so-and-so.'

'Why?' I says, 'he's not a bad lad. He just wants a bit of handling.'

One of them was this young player, Jackie Benbow, of Rovers; he'd been sent off four times before he was twenty, and every referee had an eye out for him. Some people said it was a case of giving a dog a bad name, because of the way he wore his hair; it was blond and long at the back and kind of pointed in that duck's backside, or whatever you call the style, though as far as I'm concerned, that sort of thing doesn't make any difference.

He was a funny youngster, really, because off the field you wouldn't think he'd say boo to a goose; he was so shy he'd hardly ever open his mouth. Another thing was he was really a very good player, a centre-forward, he didn't *need* to be rough, because he had all the ball control.

Well, the first time *I* ever refereed him, he did something in the first ten minutes, and I called him over to me and said, the next time you do that, son, I'm taking your name.

I remember I was surprised because he didn't say anything; just looked at me with a sort of expression as if he couldn't understand it. Halfway through the second half, he was going through for a goal and one of the full-backs came across and slide-tackled him. It was a perfectly good tackle, he took the ball, but when Benbow got up, he deliberately tripped him, he took his feet away. 'Right,' I said, and I got out my notebook. Some referees get it out to threaten a player, but not me, I believe that weakens your authority. If you get it out, you've got to mean it.

'All right,' I said, 'what's your name, son?' and he didn't answer me, he was just sort of staring at me, like he had before. 'You heard me,' I said, 'what's your name?'

Of course, I knew his name all right, but you've got to go through with the formality, and if you ask him his name, he's got to tell you, otherwise you're letting him get away with it. I don't believe in all this turning a player round and looking at the number on his back.

He still didn't speak, so I said, 'Come on, you're holding up the game;' then he looked away from me and he said, 'You know my name.'

'Never mind whether I know it or not,' I said, 'if I ask you, you've got to give it me.' Then he went all red all over his face as if something had embarrassed him, and he mumbled it. I could just make out the 'Benbow', and I wrote it down and I said, 'All right, the next time, you're off.'

I didn't see him again that season, the next time was about September, a midweek game against the Wolves at Molineux. Early on, after a tackle, I saw him turn round and say something to the centre-half, so I ran along beside him – I always believe in that, so long as it's nothing serious – and I said, 'You know me, son, and I know you. Just keep your mouth shut till after the game.' The rest of the match, he was as good as gold.

Well that's it, I thought. He's learning. He's no different to the rest of them, no worse and no better. If he sees you mean what you say, he'll behave himself.

I had him again three weeks later, this time up in the North in a home match, and there wasn't a thing. After that, I used to read now and again about his being in this incident and that incident, but I didn't blame him, basically, I blamed the referees. It's always the same in football; you keep turning your back on the little things, and sooner or later you get a big thing; somebody blows his top and there's trouble, not only for the player, but for the referee as well. The League don't like it if you get involved in too many disciplinary committees, and the F. A. notice it, too. I mean it tells its own story, doesn't it?

It wasn't till Christmas I refereed him again, Christmas morning, at Everton, I saw him in the passage there, when I came in. 'Hallo, Benbow,' I said, going past, 'happy Christmas,' but he's slow, the boy, very slow, he just sort of looked at me with his mouth open, and I was in my dressing-room before he'd had time to answer.

It was a hard game, and quite a good one; both sides were in the running for the title, so both of them needed the points.

*Football Crazy*

I remember Benbow headed a goal, a very nice one, and it was the first time I'd ever seen him smile, then Everton equalized, and with ten minutes to the end, it was still one-all.

Then Benbow got a ball just beyond the centre circle, he took it past a couple of men, lovely footwork, and it looked as if he'd go right through when the third one brought him down. Benbow got up, and he took a kick at him.

'All right,' I said, 'off!' and I pointed towards the dressing-room. Well, I had them all round me in a minute, swarming all round me, Benbow, the captain, two or three of the others. Benbow kept saying, 'It was him! He tripped me!' and he had that same expression on, I recognized it, like the time I took his name, as if he couldn't understand what he'd done wrong. 'Off!' I said. 'Go on!' because if there's one thing I won't have on the field, it's kicking, provocation or no provocation. Let it go, and there's no knowing what you'll have on your hands.

Well, when I got on to the train afterwards, the first person I see, sitting all on his own in a corner of the carriage, is Benbow. He saw me as well, I could tell that by the way he tried to turn his face away, but as far as I'm concerned that sort of thing's silly; when a match is over, it's over, and besides, I wanted to give him a bit of advice. So I went into the compartment and I sat down beside him and I said, 'Hallo, where are *you* going?'

He didn't look at me, he just mumbled something which sounded like, 'Home'. I knew he was a Yorkshire boy, so I reckoned they'd let him off, because they were playing at Sheffield next day.

'Well,' I said, 'that was a silly thing you did,' and he said something again, but so quiet you couldn't hear him, and I leaned over close and I said, 'What?' and this time I could just about make it out, he said, 'I didn't *do* nothing.'

'Of course you did,' I said. 'You kicked him. You don't think I'd send you off for nothing. Now look here, son, you're being a fool to yourself. You want to play for England, don't you? Well, *don't* you?' and he said he did.

'Well, what do you think the selectors think when they read

about you being sent off, or having your name taken? You don't think they're going to take a chance with you, especially abroad, do you? If you kick somebody abroad you'll bring the house down. Eh?'

But as I've said, he was a funny lad, it was hard to get an answer from him, he'd go into himself like a shell.

'Listen,' I said, 'have a bit of sense, you'll be suspended for this, you'll probably get a fortnight. You'll lose money, your club have got to play without you, and you're that much farther from getting an England cap. You may have been provoked, I'm not saying you weren't, but as soon as you do anything like that, you put yourself in the wrong, and if you go on doing it, you'll spoil your whole career; I'll tell you, I've seen it happen before. All right, that's enough of that, I'm going out to have my tea. Are you coming?'

He just shook his head, and by the time I got back, he'd disappeared. Still, he seemed to remember what I said, because I must have refereed him four or five times over the next year, and there was never any trouble at all. He got fourteen days suspension for the Everton match, like I told him he would, but in those games, I don't remember even giving a foul against him. So when I read now and again about his having his name taken, or when other referees used to complain to me about him, I just used to laugh to myself, because as far as I was concerned, I could tell it was six of one and half a dozen of the other.

Early this season, I took Rovers' game against Sheffield Wednesday.

It was a tough game, both sides going hard, and just about on the half-hour, there was a dust-up, nothing very serious, between Benbow and one of the Wednesday defence. I went over there and I said, 'Look, son, you remember me, we want none of that today.' And the next thing he did was he hit me, he hit me right below the eye; he was walking off the field before I'd even got up off the ground.

*Sine die* suspension he got for that. He'll be lucky if he ever plays again, *I* can tell you.

# The Ref's a Woman!

*Paul Wilson*

Cayline Vincent, a 23-year-old New Zealander, has plenty of the Amy Johnson spirit, but is beginning to wonder why she did not set her heart on something as straightforward as transatlantic flying.

Instead, she decided to pursue a career as a rugby league referee, which in aviatrix terms is like trying to circle the globe through anti-aircraft fire.

She was good enough to make the A-grade in her local league within four years of taking up the sport, but, frustrated at reaching a ceiling at that level, she came to England this season to further her experience.

To her disappointment, she found the most she could hope for were amateur fixtures and occasional chances to run the line at Alliance level, lower grade appointments than she had been used to. Worse, the resentment and resistance met in this country was far greater than in her home state of North Queensland.

'Australia isn't exactly famous for enlightened attitudes to women, but ideas here are 10 years behind the times,' said Vincent, billeted in Castleford. 'People are very set in their ways. Men regard rugby league as their game.'

The weekend brings another amateur match, Staincliff v Corkickle in the National Cup. The type of tie, she says which someone is bound to describe as an odd choice for a rookie referee. 'I'm more qualified than most refs at that level, though I admit I didn't quite know what to expect at first,' she said. 'When I did my first BARLA game, it had to be explained to me that there wasn't going to be a crowd, there were no proper touch judges, and I couldn't use the sin-bin.

'Without those three supports it was quite intimidating being in the middle of 26 lads knocking hell out of each other. Some of the sides here are pretty undisciplined, but some want to play. I'd sooner talk than use the whistle all the time, and most seem to respect that.'

Overt intimidation on the field has not so far been a problem, unlike in Australia, where she was once hit in the face by an ungallant young man called Adrian Salt. Over here, she maintains, the aggro comes from fellow officials, not players.

'One grade two referee from

## The Ref's a Woman!

Hull came up to me, after I'd run the line in an Alliance match, and accused me of doing a bloke out of a game,' she said. 'I'd just taken a freezing cold shower, to be out of the way before the others arrived, and he added that if I thought I was a man I shouldn't expect privacy.

'I don't, if they want to be like that about it, but I would rather make a name as a referee. I can't possibly be a threat to all these men because I'm returning to Australia eventually, and I can't see women getting to take First Division games in my time of service.

'I started doing this because I love the game and enjoy a challenge, but I'm sick of fighting for everything,' she said. 'All I ask before I return is an Alliance match, just to prove my worth.' Less hopefully, she added: 'I've been told it's up to Fred Lindop.'

Over Easter, Vincent will travel to The Netherlands with Hornsey Lambs, the north London club she refereed in the last round of the BARLA Amateur Cup, and whose second-round match against Elland takes place on Sunday at the New River Sports Centre, White Hart Lane.

Isobel Reid, connected with Hornsey, has observed Vincent's mounting disappointment. 'I don't think Cayline bargained for the amount of prejudice she was going to run into,' she said. 'It's a pity the game has such a blind spot about women, because in other respects, such as the way racism is not tolerated, it's very healthy.

'Women tend to like rugby league – it's less loutish than football – but we get the idea that men want to keep it exactly like it is, exactly where it is.'

## *Sports at School*

# The Screams of the Damned

*Adèle Geras*

They've sent me back to school, even though there's nothing for me to do here. I'm sitting in the reference library now, and I can hear the shouts of all the poor unfortunates careering round the playing fields. The screams of the damned, I call it, although they are probably enjoying themselves hugely. I'm very relieved to be done with games. They always seemed to me a particularly unrefined method of torture.

Consider:
1 Bare knees, and a high wind straight off the sea. Rain too, quite often.
2 Mud beneath your feet, infiltrating your shoes and squelching in your socks.
3 A lot of hard sticks that could catch you (and did catch you) painful blows on shins, ankles, and knees.
4 An unpredictable ball that could go anywhere, and that you had to follow, even though everyone else was chasing it, so whatever was the point in getting yourself crushed in the fray?
5 Ordinary classmates transformed into wild-eyed viragos, hair disheveled, panting, shouting at you because what you were doing was wrong.
6 Mrs Williams of the shiny eyes and healthy cheeks yelling: 'Come on, Flora. Buck up, Run,' as she passed you with a leap, pleated shorts flying and red knees flashing above navy-blue socks.

That's the winter. In the summer, there's cricket. Nothing pleasanter, nothing more evocative of hearts at peace under an

## The Screams of the Damned

English heaven than the thwack of leather on willow, or is it vice-versa? It's all right if you're wearing a straw hat with long, pink satin ribbons and sitting in the shade of an ancient tree, waiting for tea and sandwiches in the pavilion, as you watch elegant young men (fair-haired, of course, and noble-browed, every last one of them) in immaculate whites running between the wickets. It's quite another thing to be stuck out in the deep field, waiting hours for someone to send a ball in your direction, then throwing it in so badly that mid-wicket has to retrieve it, and the other side is clocking up runs at an alarming rate. Batting is even worse. There you are, minding your own business, when some demon bowler with meaty thighs bowls a red cannonball straight at you with terrifying speed, and you are supposed to play forward and hit the blasted thing, and with a straight bat, what's more. Every instinct says: 'Run away,' but that's not cricket, as the saying goes, so you make a feeble gesture in the direction of the lethal scarlet projectile and lean your body as far as possible away from it, praying very hard. Even if you hit it, your troubles aren't over. You sometimes have to run, and I've always regarded running as a complete waste of time, unless there's a bus to be caught.

*Sports at School*

# That Showed 'em

*Roger Mills*

That public school ideal 'A healthy body and a healthy mind' was another bee in the school's comprehensive bonnet. But they had decided that two periods of P.E. and an afternoon of games was enough for the body part of it – plus all the help medical science could give us of course.

Every year for the first three years we had a medical examination in which our eyes, ears and mouths were checked for typhoid, whooping cough, tetanus, diptheria and polio. It was a brief but thorough examination culminating in that final embarrassing 'cough'.

The second year however threatened extras in the form of T.B. injections. There were two injections starting with one to discover if you needed the other. The first was a minor affair which caused a little bump to appear briefly on the forearm. The actual T.B. needle itself, the older boys told us, was a horrendous instrument of torture. It was by all accounts a long spike with a little spiked wheel around it. When the spike was jabbed into your arm the smaller spikes made contact and then, controlled like an egg whisk, the wheel revolved and burrowed a circular bloody moat around the central spike.

Lining up for this, boys passed out, turned a milky white and if of a religious nature prayed. None of the rumours were true of course, it was a clean painless jab. I had not believed the stories anyway – much.

It was like checking the health of the man to be hanged. It was all to make sure that we would survive the onslaught of the 'Games' they were to bombard us with.

Immediately after tutor group on alternative Thursdays we bundled into a coach outside the school and set off for Epping

# That Showed 'Em

Lodge, a snooty sports centre which condescended to let us run riot. In our bags we carried the prescribed kit, all washed, scrubbed and ironed by our mothers the night before: white vest and shorts, socks, plimsoles and towel.

In the summer, games provided a pleasant interlude away from school. Come the winter however we saw the snow white streets on the journey and knew it was useless even hoping for a bit of sunshine. It was too late for that. Instead we would wish for an arctic snowflood inches thick covering up the playing fields so that 'Games' would be abandoned. But it never happened. Come sleet, hail and thunderstorms we still had to take off our clothes and run about outside. Jamie, Paul and I always did the same sports together. We played tennis in the first, football in the second and even had a go at archery and shinty. Shinty is the game where you bash each other with wonky sticks.

I was never really good at sports. I was capable physically but I could not stand the competition...

... If I was not very good at games generally I was terrible at football. I could run and pass but spent the whole game avoiding the ball because I could not tackle and was frightened of being laughed at. I was always last to be picked for teams and was the booby prize for whichever team got me. It was in the last five minutes of the last game I ever played that I got my triumph and revenge.

The team I was in scored such a disputed goal that the P.E. master let the opposing team choose who they wanted of our team to take the penalty. Of course they chose me.

Paul lined up the ball for me in front of the goal and the two teams stood away from its mouth while I prepared myself. I checked the wind direction, ground condition and reviewed the situation. Everybody's eyes were on me and everything went very quiet. Behind the goal, getting smaller all the time, I could see the other groups returning to the showers. I knew this kick would be the last one, on this we either won or drew.

'Now should I place it in the top of the net where this giant goalkeeper might get at it or should I try to trick him by making it look like I was going to kick it one way and then kick it the other . . . ' The hell with it, I just booted it. The ball soared higher than I had ever kicked it before and entered the goal in the top right hand corner. The goalie made a dive for it but didn't stand a chance.

There was a moment's silence while everybody's mind flipped back a bit to verify that they had really seen me score. Action-Replay.

'Yea that showed 'em,' came Jamie's exhilarated cry from behind, and he was on the other side. It was a nice end to my soccer career and rather than return to the obscurity of left-back I decided to take up cross-country running.

# Skivers

*David Williams*

**Characters**

Claire Morton         *14 years old*
Paula Wood            *Claire's friend*
Helen Clark           *A class-mate*
Miss Dunn             *Their Games Teacher*
Reporter
Announcer

*(Exterior acoustic. A whistle blows)*

**Miss Dunn:** Right girls. Everybody line up behind the flags, please.

*(Crowded commotion)*

Don't push. Spread yourselves right down the track.

**Helen:** Not fair, miss. The ones at the front get a start on us.

**Miss Dunn:** It's four miles, Helen. I'm sure you'll catch up.

**Claire:** *(Mimicking)* Not fair, miss.

**Paula:** What house is she in?

**Claire:** Who cares? This is stupid.

**Paula:** I don't see why everybody has to run. Why don't they just let the Helen Clarks an' them get on with it. They'll win anyway. We could just stay and cheer.

**Claire:** Wouldn't cheer that stuck-up tart.

**Miss Dunn:** Claire Morton! What are you doing with your coat on?

*Sports at School*

**Claire:** It's freezing, miss.

**Miss Dunn:** Don't be stupid. You can't run in that.

**Claire:** Don't want to run.

**Miss Dunn:** Take it off.

**Claire:** Nowhere to put it.

**Miss Dunn:** Give it here. What House are you in?

**Claire:** Tyne.

**Miss Dunn:** So why didn't you pick up a yellow band. We won't be able to tell who you're running for.

**Claire:** I'm not running for anybody.

**Miss Dunn:** Nonsense. Well, it's too late now. Get into line. You too, Paula Wood. *(Calling)* Everybody ready?

*(Gun fires. A stampede)*

**Claire:** *(Running)* Hang on, Paula. Don't run so rotten fast.

**Paula:** I'm getting carried away with the rest.

**Claire:** We'll be carried off if we keep this pace up. Four miles an' we're not out the gate yet.

**Paula:** Helen Clark is.

**Claire:** Slow down.

**Paula:** We're last now.

**Claire:** Good. That way nobody'll see us skiving off.

**Paula:** How d'you mean?

**Claire:** My house is just round the corner. Let's nip in there for a cup of coffee.

**Paula:** We can't do that. We'll be miles behind.

**Claire:** They come back the same way, stupid. We'll just tuck in behind them. Nobody'll know.

**Paula:** I don't . . .

**Claire:** What's the problem?

**Paula:** I don't want people calling me a cheat . . .

**Claire:** They won't know. Anyway, it's not as if we're trying to win. We're going to be last in any case, so what's the diff . . . Come on, if you're that keen on running I'll race you to my house.

*(Fade running. Interior acoustic. Coffee pours)*

**Claire:** Want a top-up?

**Paula:** Thanks.

**Claire:** There's some chocolate biscuits in that tin.

**Paula:** Shouldn't really but . . . go on, then. What sort do you want? Marathon?

**Claire:** Very clever.

**Paula:** Funny how half these biscuits have got sporty names, but all they do is make you fat, not fit.

**Claire:** And spotty.

**Paula:** We should be doing that run, you know. Good for you. Helen Clark's very slim.

**Claire:** Skinny. Anyway, what came first? Is she thin because she runs or does she run because she's thin?

**Paula:** Yeah, I see what you mean. I suppose you feel like it more if you've got the figure for it.

**Claire:** That's why I hate sport, me. I look gross in Games stuff. And it's always so rotten cold.

*Sports at School*

**Paula:** Showers are the worst thing. Why do they always make you go in the showers?

**Claire:** 'Cause they're all sadists, Gym teachers.

**Paula:** D'you reckon?

**Claire:** Mollie Dunn is anyway.

**Paula:** Wouldn't be surprised.

**Claire:** You know she used to be a javelin thrower? Professional, sort of. I bet she was one o' them what took drugs. Changed her hormones. Bet she's a man underneath.

**Paula:** I hope she's not checking everybody's out on the course. She does that sometimes in Games, drives round the route in that old Volkswagen ticking people off.

**Claire:** Not today, though. Not with parents round an' all, and trophies to sort out. It's all official business today. She loves that, swaggering about. Want some more coffee?

**Paula:** I'll sound just like a washing machine when I get up. Half a cup, that's all. Yeah, there was quite a crowd at the finish last year. I wonder what it's like to come in first. You know, in front of the whole school. Be the winner and get presented with the trophy and everything.

**Claire:** You're starting to sound like Helen Clark.

**Paula:** She got her name in the papers last time she won it.

**Claire:** The Tyne Valley News. Big deal.

**Paula:** More than you've ever done, I dare say.

**Claire:** Our Gavin was in the paper once, that time him and Terry Bowles got fined for pinching a car. But they never printed their names 'cause they were under-age or summat. So you wouldn't know it was him unless you knew it was him.

**Paula:** Eh?

**Claire:** What time is it?

**Paula:** Dunno. Left my watch with Dunnie. Has your mam not got a clock?

**Claire:** Our Gavin broke it. D'you reckon they'll be coming back yet?

**Paula:** No idea. How long does it take to run four miles?

**Claire:** Well, people talk about doing a mile in four minutes, don't they?

**Paula:** That's proper athletes.

**Claire:** Say five minutes, then. Five-and-a-half maybe. So four times five-and-a-half is . . . what? Better say six. Six times four.

**Paula:** Twenty four.

**Claire:** The brains of the girl. And how long do you think we've skived off in here?

**Paula:** At least half an hour, I'd say.

**Claire:** We'd better get a move on, then. It's all right being last but we don't want to make it look as if we've walked all the way.

**Paula:** We haven't even done that. Tell you what, let's run back from here. Then we might look as if we've done four miles. OK?

**Claire:** Don't know about that, I got a stitch when we ran before. You're hard to keep up with when you start.

**Paula:** Come on.

**Claire:** (*Reluctantly*) Right.

*(Fade. Exterior acoustic. Running.)*

**Paula:** (*Calling*) Come on, I could walk quicker.

*Sports at School*

**Claire:** It's all that coffee. Like greyhounds.

**Paula:** Eh?

**Claire:** *(Catching up, out of breath)* Greyhounds. Me dad used to reckon when they wanted to keep a favourite from winning they'd give it a massive bowl o' water just before the start. Then they'd back the second favourite.

**Paula:** What a cheat.

**Claire:** Clever, though. Undetectable. Just like us.

**Paula:** I hope so. I keep looking out for Dunnie's car.

**Claire:** Relax. There's nobody about.

**Paula:** I know we must be miles behind. They'll all have gone home by now.

**Claire:** So what. Do you want people to see you trail in last?

**Paula:** Oh, there's some left anyway. See, there's the field.

**Claire:** Never thought I'd be pleased to see school.

**Paula:** There's quite a few, look. They must have all had to stay to see the last ones in.

**Claire:** Serves them right.

**Paula:** I wonder who won?

**Claire:** Who's bothered?

**Paula:** House points an' that. I think Helen Clark's in Tees. I'm in Tees.

**Claire:** I'm in coffees.

**Paula:** Coffee's in me.

**Claire:** Good, that. What's the other one we say? It wasn't the cough that carried me off . . .

**Paula:** It was the coffin they carried me off in.

**Claire:** God, we're funny, us. We're like them two women on telly.

**Paula:** We'll be famous one day.

*(Faint crowd noise)*

**Claire:** Listen to that lot cheering. I bet we get a bigger cheer than the winners.

**Paula:** See, I said we'd be famous. Come on, let's give 'em a big finish!

**Claire:** Yea . . . ah!

*(Running hard as the cheers get louder, encouraged by an indistinct tannoy annoucement. The noise rises to a climax, followed by applause.)*

**Paula:** Beat you!

**Claire:** Did not! We went through the tape together.

**Paula:** What did you say?

**Claire:** We both broke the tape.

**Paula:** What tape?

**Claire:** Are you blind as well as daft? The tape they had stretched across the track.

**Paula:** But that's only for . . .

**Reporter:** Well done, girls. Well done. I didn't catch your names on the tannoy. There's a Claire, isn't there? Which one of you's Claire?

**Claire:** Who wants to know?

**Reporter:** Tyne Valley News. Bob, get a shot of these two while they're still puffing. That'll make a better picture than the prize-giving.

*Sports at School*

**Paula:** Prize-giving?

**Announcer:** And just coming into view in third place, it looks like last year's winner, Helen Clark. Give Helen a big cheer as she comes in.

*(Cheers from the crowd)*

**Claire:** Hey Paula, Helen Clark's just third. She'll be sick as a chip. Wonder who beat her.

**Paula:** We did, you stupid twit!

**Claire:** What?

**Paula:** We've beaten her! Do you not realize what we've gone an' done? We've come in first and second!

**Reporter:** Dead heat, I'd say. Hope so. That'll make quite a good story. Are you two friends, at all?

**Paula:** You and your four-minute miles.

**Claire:** You're the one who added it all up, brainpan.

**Paula:** Don't blame me. If you had a stupid clock in your house . . .

**Reporter:** Hey girls, you've just won the big race. What's all the fuss?

**Claire:** That's right! We've just won the race. What are we arguing about? We're gonna get our names in the paper. I'm Claire with an 'i' by the way. This is Paula.

**Miss Dunn:** Claire Morton and Paula Woods, come over here.

**Paula:** We're for it now.

**Miss Dunn:** I'd like to know how you two managed to come in ahead of the rest.

**Claire:** We're on drugs, miss.

42

**Miss Dunn:** Don't you be funny with me. If I hear you've been taking a short cut . . .

**Paula:** We never took any short cuts, honest.

**Miss Dunn:** You've never run anything like as fast as this before.

**Reporter:** What's that? Personal best for both of them, is it?

**Miss Dunn:** Who are you?

**Reporter:** I'm from the Tyne Valley News. You must coach these girls, do you?

**Miss Dunn:** Well, I . . .

**Reporter:** Bob, let's have a picture over here with these two girls and their trainer. Get in the middle there Mrs . . . er . . .

**Miss Dunn:** Mollie Dunn. Miss, actually, Well, Ms. If you put Ms . . .

**Helen:** *(Approaching)* Miss!

**Miss Dunn:** Not just now, Helen.

**Helen:** Miss, this isn't fair.

**Miss Dunn:** I said, not now! *(To Reporter)* How would you like me to stand? Should I have my arms round the girls like this?

**Reporter:** Very cosy. Got that, Bob? Great. Thanks a lot.

**Miss Dunn:** Let me take you over to meet the Head. He'll be pleased to hear there's a good story about the school going in the News for a change.

**Reporter:** O.K. See you later, girls.

**Helen:** Miss Dunn . . .

**Miss Dunn:** Not now, Helen.

**Claire:** *(To Paula)* What a laugh, eh?

*Sports at School*

**Paula:** We'll be in real bother over this.

**Claire:** No we won't. Dunnie wants her picture in the paper. 'Coach Congratulates Winning Pair', that sort o' thing.

**Paula:** More like 'Cheat Row At School Sports'.

**Claire:** Dunnie'll shut Helen Clark up. And who's to prove we didn't win fair and square?

**Paula:** But we didn't.

**Claire:** We might have done if we tried. We finished pretty fast.

**Paula:** Don't be so stupid.

**Claire:** Hey, the look on Helen Clark's face when she found she was third . . .

**Paula:** She had a good right. It's not fair.

**Claire:** You're sounding like her again. Listen, I reckon it's not fair that she gets stacks of medals all the time and we end up wi' nowt. So what if she misses a prize for once in her life? It's the only one I'll ever get. An' what about you? Your mam'll be right proud when she sees your picture in the paper.

**Paula:** But there's nothing to be proud about, is there? We should be ashamed of ourselves.

**Claire:** So what you gonna do about it? Run after than reporter and tell him the truth?

**Paula:** Maybe.

**Claire:** And who's gonna thank you for that, apart from snot-faced Clark? Dunnie won't. The Head definitely won't. Your mam and dad won't. Who you trying to please? God?

**Announcer:** The award ceremony will begin in two minutes. Would the winners please report to the rostrum now.

**Claire:** Come on, Paula. Let's go an' be famous.

**Paula:** I know what I'm going to do.

**Claire:** Where you off to? We're wanted back there.

**Paula:** You go if you like. I've got four miles to run.

**Claire:** Oh no.

**Paula:** *(Running)* Are you coming or not?

**Announcer:** Would Claire Morton and Paula Wood please report to the rostrum.

**Claire:** *(Calling)* Paula! We're wanted. *(Muttering)* Stupid tart. I'll never speak to you again. *(Calling)* Paula! Paula! Hang on. Wait for me. Don't run so rotten fast!

*(Fade out on running)*

*Sports at School*

# After Sports Day

*John Foster*

Stung by the taunting laughter
As I panted in last,
Having been forced to take part
So as not to let the side down,
I climbed to the top of the chestnut
And tearfully vowed
That no son of mine
Would run against his will.

Why is it
That twenty years on
I feel a father's pride,
Watching my son
Come striding first to the finish,
Forgetting the agony
Of the forlorn figure
Trailing in
Last?

# Aliens

*Brian Keaney*

All my comic-book heroes played football, from Roy of the Rovers to Ted Legge in the *Valiant*. It was what the kids played in the streets and in the car-parks. We played it in the playground at school with tennis balls which were always getting lost or nicked by older kids. I loved football. Mind you, I don't pretend that I was brilliant at it. I would never play for England or for Ireland (which was my secret dream) but I was good enough at it and I enjoyed playing it. I was always a pretty skinny kid, but you don't need to be built like a bull to be good at it. The less physical contact there is in football, the better the play. You risk the odd bruised shin but it's worth it.

In a game of rugby, on the other hand, you risk your life, especially the way they played it at our school. I hated rugby. I absolutely loathed it, but of course we had to play it at our stupid school, because we were a grammar school. In other words, the headmaster dreamed that he was in charge of a public school, so football was forbidden. It was much too working class.

For a start, I could never understand the rules of rugby. Knock-ons and line-outs, five-yard scrums and drop-kicks. It all sounded like a different language to me. And all that physical contact. Bending down and putting your arms round the others. That I did not like at all. Now if ours had been a mixed school, I might have felt differently.

Our rugby master loved all that: the freezing cold pitches, the grazed knees, the huddled boys. He was a right sadist, if you ask me. He was the head of the cadet force at our school, and he was exactly the same in or out of uniform, barking orders at you left, right and centre. His name was Mr Dougan but everybody called him the Commandant. He had all sorts of punishments of his own for boys he did not like. When he took you for PE, he would

## Sports at School

hit you with one of the climbing ropes if he felt like it. But that wasn't as bad as being made to run round and round the playing fields in the middle of winter in just a pair of shorts. He disliked anyone who wasn't absolutely fanatical about rugby. But most of all he hated anyone who tried to get out of doing it. If you brought a note from your parents to say that you'd had both your legs shot off the night before, he would still look at you in utter disbelief.

'Well, we wouldn't like to strain ourselves,' he would sneer. 'Must be careful, mustn't we?' He'd go on like this for ages until suddenly, tiring of it, he would give you some really awful job to do, like picking up all the stones on pitch number three, which was a bit like telling you to polish a battleship with a toothbrush. So it was a choice between playing rugby or freezing to death and getting backache.

What made it worse was that my best friend, Kevin Seer, was pretty good at rugby. Not only that, but he actually admitted to me that he liked it. 'Honestly, Brian,' he said, 'it's a brilliant game. You ought to give it a try.'

'What do you mean, give it a try?' I said. 'What do you think I do every Thursday out on the playing fields, meditate?'

'Oh, come off it,' Kevin said. 'You don't really put any effort into it, do you?'

'Effort into it?' I said. 'You must be mad. I put an enormous amount of effort into steering clear of lunatics like you, charging about like a lot of stampeding rhinos.'

Kevin looked at me like he thought I was pathetic. 'Honestly, Brian,' he said, 'You're turning into a right weed.'

Well, he could say what he liked. I wasn't going to take any notice of it. As far as I was concerned, anybody who played rugby for fun had to have something pretty seriously wrong with their brain. I told him so as well.

'You're turning into a right moron, Kevin,' I said. 'Charging about the pitch, bashing into people. I suppose that's the bit you enjoy.'

Kevin didn't say anything. He just walked off. The thing was,

Kevin wasn't a bit like that, really. He wasn't one of those people who enjoy hurting people. Not like Kennedy. Kennedy was captain of the third-year team. He was a massive kid. Even the sixth-formers were frightened of him. Only the week before he had had a fight with O'Conner who was a fifth-former and fancied himself as a bit of a hard nut.

I'd wandered into the toilet at break, not expecting anything unusual and there, to my amazement, was a whole ring of kids and in the middle were Kennedy and O'Conner, beating the living daylights out of each other. O'Conner was quite a bit older and taller than Kennedy so you would have thought it would be no contest, but Kennedy didn't seem to care how much he got hit, he just kept wading in like a robot. After a while O'Conner began to look worried. Suddenly Kennedy was getting the upper hand. O'Conner was looking desperately around him now. It was like a dam had burst. Kennedy was just punching and punching, and O'Conner was doing absolutely nothing but soak it up. There was blood all over the place. It seemed to be coming from O'Conner's mouth and nose. Anybody else would have stopped but Kennedy just kept on hitting him and hitting him. O'Conner collapsed on the floor and Kennedy started to kick him. God knows what would have happened if I hadn't suddenly shouted, 'Teacher!' Kids began rushing out of the toilet, myself among them. I just couldn't bear it any longer.

Of course, the Commandant loved Kennedy. He acted like Kennedy was his own son. Even the headmaster was forever spouting about him at assembly, and how well the third-year team was doing under his captaincy.

Kevin wasn't a bit like that. He never picked fights. I suppose he could have defended himself against most of the others, but he wasn't interested. But one thing that he and Kennedy had in common was the look that came into their faces when they were playing rugby. It was the look of the kamikaze pilot. The kill-or-be-killed look of absolute dedication. I suppose that's what the troops looked like going over the trenches in the First World War, or what the Vikings looked like when they came charging

## Sports at School

out of their longboats and went off raping and pillaging. It was the look of sheer lunacy, in my opinion.

There were three rugby pitches. Two of them were used every Thursday by us, and the third was kept for matches against other schools. We were divided up into two groups of thirty. Kennedy and the First Fifteen played on pitch one against another fifteen made up of hopefuls who wanted to get into the school team. It was this that Kevin was trying for, and there was no doubt that sooner or later he would be transferred upwards. In the meantime, he had to put up with the rest of us on pitch two. The Commandant always chose him to pick a side. The other team captain was always a big fat kid called Bates. He was a horrible looking kid, he wobbled when he walked, but he was powerful and surprisingly fast.

You'd have thought that Kevin would have picked me to be in his team. After all, we were supposed to be friends; but, oh no, he took it much too seriously for that. And of course Bates didn't want me either so I was always left till right at the end, when, amid groans from his team-mates, one of the captains would reluctantly say, 'I suppose we'll have Keaney.'

Well, I didn't care if they didn't want me in the team. I didn't want to play in the first place. The Commandant would give me a look like he absolutely hated my guts and blow the whistle for the game to start. Up on pitch one there was no referee. It was just assumed that being the school team and a bunch of their admirers, they would do the decent thing and play by the rules. What it really meant, in fact, was that Kennedy was in charge and if anybody didn't think his tactics were entirely fair, all they had to do was say so. In return he would rearrange their faces for them. And this was the game that Kevin was eating his heart out to join!

I always played on the wing. It wasn't too bad when spring came and the weather improved. It was terrible in the middle of winter. Nobody ever passed to me. I had dropped so many catches that it was generally accepted that passing the ball to Keaney was a sure way of giving the other side three points.

You see, the thing about rugby that I could never get on with was the ridiculous shape of the ball. I mean, how on earth are you supposed to play a sensible game with a ball shaped like that? You can never tell where it's going to go.

So I wasn't really a part of the team at all. I just ran about vaguely in the same direction as the rest of them and day-dreamed. It wasn't too bad really. Except once.

It was a crisp spring morning. The ground was all covered with frost; your breath came out in front of you like smoke; the sort of morning the Commandant loved. He was charging up and down in his rugby shirt and shorts, barking out orders as usual. 'Come on, hurry up. Let's get started. Stop talking, you lot. Right, everybody in a group here, come on, where are the captains? Blah, blah, blah.' All it meant was that the game took twice as long to start because he wouldn't shut up and let the kids organize themselves.

I was second to last to be chosen this time, beaten only by Weedy Wilkinson. What a disgrace, to be reckoned with that little twerp! Still, I didn't really care. I quickly went and took up my position on the wing. The surface of the pitch looked like another planet to me. It was all frozen into ridges, the grass was like rows of little spears. I looked at the other players jogging up and down on the pitch. I began day-dreaming again.

*This is planetary ecologist Keaney reporting back to Mothership. This is the most extraordinary planet I have yet discovered. It seems to be inhabited by a bizarre, semi-humanoid life form. They are divided into two kinds, clearly distinguishable by colourful markings. They seem to communicate mainly by signs or grunts, and there is one of them who appears to be the leader and makes high-pitched whistling noises.*

*The herd instinct seems very strong amongst these creatures. They stick together, sometimes even performing a strange dance which involves them huddling together in a regular formation. There is another, similar dance which requires them to form into two lines. Both these rituals, and indeed most of their behaviour, seems to revolve around a large, brown, oval object, presumably an egg, which is passed continually from one to the other.*

*I am convinced that this is some sort of religious ritual, since I can see no logical reason for this behaviour...*

Suddenly my day-dreaming was shattered. The players were all rushing towards me at horrible speed. I heard my name shouted and the ball came hurtling towards me. I put my hands out and caught it. There simply wasn't time to think.

It was like standing in the fast lane of the M1. Players were coming at me from all sides at about a hundred miles an hour. There was only one thing to do: run.

I ran like the wind, swerving this way and that to avoid bodies intent on my destruction. I could hear my team shouting encouragement. It all seemed so easy. There were the posts in front of me. I swerved around one more player. It was Kevin, I realized, as I side-stepped neatly and placed the ball directly between the two posts.

You should have heard the cheers. Even the Commandant walked over and slapped me on the back. 'Well run, Keaney,' he said. I felt really pleased with myself: proud, I suppose. Perhaps there was something in this game after all. Bates put the ball down in front of the posts and converted. Another cheer went up and we returned to the centre of the pitch.

It's a wonderful feeling being a hero. I felt all sort of glowing and brave. I could see the others looking at me as if they realized how much they'd misjudged me. Quite right too, I thought, ranking me along with Weedy Wilkinson.

They kicked off again and the ball went straight into touch. We all ran down and formed up for a line out. I was really enjoying myself now, jumping up and down on my toes, waiting for the action to start again.

The ball came out of the line-out to our side, and it was quickly passed along the line of players until suddenly, there it was, flying towards me again. I put my hands out and felt it thud against my chest.

There I was, back on the M1 with the juggernauts rushing towards me at a hundred miles an hour, but I was ready for them. I streaked off down the wing, the adrenalin rushing round my system, pumping my legs up and down. I felt like I was flying as I swerved this way and that, running round opposing players who dived too late at my heels.

I could hear the others shouting, encouraging me on. 'Come on, Keaney, run!' Right in front of me I could see the posts. 'Here comes try number two,' I said to myself. It was almost too easy.

Suddenly a dark streak shot into my line of vision. Something stopped me running. It was as if my legs had caught in a rope. The rest of my body went hurtling forward and upwards. I flew through the air and came down on my head. The last thing I remember was the whistle blowing.

When I came to, the Commandant was standing over me. At first I couldn't make out what was happening. Why was I lying in bed with the Commandant standing over me? Then I realized that I wasn't in bed. I was lying on the ground. Rather hard ground at that. I tried to stand up. It was harder that I thought. My legs were all wobbly. The other players were standing round watching. At last I got up and staggered about a bit. The Commandant began to massage the back of my neck. He must have known what he was doing because things began to come back to normal. I realized that my head hurt terribly.

'All right,' said the Commandant in what was very nearly a gentle voice. 'You're all right now.'

He turned to Kevin, who was standing with the others looking slightly guilty.

'Seer,' he said. 'Take him back to the pavilion.'

Kevin took my arm and pointed me in the direction of the pavilion. We walked away from the pitch and the game restarted.

'What happened?' I asked him.

'I tripped you up,' Kevin said. 'Sorry,' he added, not very convincingly.

'Sorry?' I said. 'You raving loony. You nearly killed me.'

## Sports at School

'I couldn't let you get a try, though,' Kevin said, as if that was a satisfactory explanation.

We sat down on the bench outside the pavilion. My head was throbbing like somebody had thrown a brick at it. For all I knew I could have permanent brain damage, but after all Kevin couldn't have let me score a try. This was my friend talking.

'You're the sort of person that causes wars,' I told him.

He looked hurt. 'It's only a game,' he said. He looked over to where the others had formed scrum. 'Hey, look,' he said. 'I'd better go back and join them. You'll be all right here, won't you?'

'Oh, yes,' I said. 'I'll be fine. I'll just sit here quietly and bleed to death. You go back and enjoy your game.'

'You're not bleeding, are you?' Kevin said.

'Oh, never mind,' I told him. 'Go back there and kill a few more of the enemy.'

Kevin got up. 'Right then,' he said, and he raced back towards the pitch.

As I watched him go it occurred to me that there are two kinds of people on this earth: those with the killer instinct and those without it. It didn't matter how nice you were in normal life, like Kevin. If you had that killer instinct, you could be transformed into a homicidal maniac just by putting on a team's colours, just by donning a uniform. Kevin had joined the others by now. From where I was sitting they looked like large, striped insects rushing about. I began to drift once again into day-dream.

*This is planetary ecologist Keaney concluding report. It seems to me that the humanoids on this planet are a dangerously unstable species, prone to displays of alarming violence for apparently trivial reasons. I must recommend that this planet is not suitable for civilization. Repeat, not suitable for civilization.*

# Feet

*Jan Mark*

Unlike the Centre Court at Wimbledon, the Centre Court at our school is the one nobody wants to play on. It is made of asphalt and has dents in it, like Ryvita. All the other courts are grass, out in the sun: Centre Court is in between the science block and the canteen and when there is a Governors' Meeting the governors use it as a car park. The sun only shines on Centre Court at noon in June and there is green algae growing round the edges. When I volunteered to be an umpire at the annual tennis tournament I might have known that I was going to end up on Centre Court.

'You'd better go on Centre Court,' said Mr Evans, 'as it's your first time. It won't matter so much if you make mistakes.' I love Mr Evans. He is so tactful and he looks like an orang-utan in his track suit. I believe myself that he swings from the pipes in the changing room but I haven't personally observed this, you understand.

He just looks as if he might enjoy swinging from things. He has very long arms. Probably he can peel bananas with his toes, which have little tufts of hair on, like beard transplants. I saw them once.

So I was sitting up in my umpire's chair, just like Wimbledon, with an official school pencil and a pad of score cards and I wasn't making any mistakes. This was mainly because they were all first-round matches, the 6–0, 6–0 kind, to get rid of the worst players. All my matches were ladies' doubles which is what you call the fifth- and sixth-year girls when they are playing tennis although not at any other time. We didn't get any spectators except some first-year boys who came to look at the legs and

*Sports at School*

things and Mr Evans, on and off, who was probably there for the same reason.

All the men's matches were on the grass courts, naturally, so I didn't see anything I wanted to see which was Michael Collier. I suppose it was the thought of umpiring Collier that made me put my name down in the first place, before I remembered about ending up on Centre Court. I could only hope that I would be finished in time for the Men's Final so that I could go and watch it because definitely Collier would be in the final. People said that it was hardly worth his while playing, really, why didn't they just give him the trophy and have done with it?

Looking back, I dare say that's what he thought, too.

So anyway, I got rid of all my ladies' doubles and sat around waiting for a mixed doubles. It was cold and windy on Centre Court since it wasn't noon in June, and I wished I had worn a sweater instead of trying to look attractive sort of in short sleeves. Sort of is right. That kind of thing doesn't fool anyone. I had these sandals too which let the draught in something rotten. I should have worn wellies. No one would have noticed. Nobody looks at feet.

After the mixed doubles which was a *fiasco* I thought of going in to get a hot drink – tea or coffee or just boiling water would have done – when I noticed this thing coming down the tramlines and trying to walk on one leg like Richard the Third only all in white.

Richard the Bride.

It was using a tennis racquet head-down as a walking stick which is not done, like cheating at cards. No gentleman would do this to his tennis racquet. This is no gentleman.

'Ho,' says this Richard the Third person. 'Me Carson. You Jane.'

This does not quite qualify as Pun of the Week because he *is* Carson and I *am* Jane. He is Alan Carson from the sixth form – only he is at Oxford now – and he would not know me from Adam only he is a neighbour and used to baby-sit with me once. This is humiliating and I don't tell people.

Carson is known to do a number of strange things and walking on one leg may be one of them for all I know so I do not remark on it.

'Hello, Carson,' I said, very coolly. I was past sounding warm, anyway. 'Where are you going?'

Carson sits down on a stacking chair at the foot of my ladder.

'I'm going to get changed,' he says.

'Did you lose your match?' I say, tactfully like Mr Evans. I am surprised because he is next most likely after Collier to be in the final.

'No, I won,' says Carson. 'But it was a Pyrrhic victory,' and he starts whanging the net post with his tennis racquet, boing boing. This is not good for it either, I should think.

I have heard about Pyrrhic victories but I do not know what they are.

'What's a Pyrrhic victory?' I said.

'One you can do without,' said Carson. 'Named after King Pyrrhus of Epirus who remarked, after beating the Romans in a battle, "One more win like this and we've had it," on account of the Romans badly chewing up his army.'

'Oh,' I said. 'And did he get another win?'

'Yes,' said Carson. 'But then he got done over at the battle of Beneventum by Curius Dentatus the famous Roman general with funny teeth. Now I just knocked spots off Pete Baldwin in the quarter-final and I'm running up to the net to thank him for a jolly good game old boy, when I turn my ankle and fall flat on my back. It's a good thing,' he added, thoughtfully, 'that I didn't get as far as the net, because I should have jumped over it and *then* fallen flat on my back.'

I could see his point. That's the kind of thing that happens to me.

'I should have met Mick Collier in the semi-final,' said Carson. 'Now he'll have a walk-over. Which should suit him. He doesn't care where he puts his feet.'

'Who will he play in the final?' I say, terribly pleased for Collier as well as being sorry for Carson whose ankle is definitely

*Sports at School*

---

swelling as even I can see without my glasses which I do not wear in between matches although everyone can see I wear them because of the red mark across my nose.

'Mills or McGarrity,' says Carson. 'Mills is currently beating McGarrity and then Collier will beat Mills – to pulp – and no one will be surprised. I don't know why we bother,' he says, tiredly. 'It was a foregone conclusion,' and he limps away, dragging his injured foot and not even trying to be funny about it because obviously it hurts like hell.

Then it started to rain.

Everybody came and sheltered in the canteen and griped, especially Mills and McGarrity, especially Mills who was within an inch of winning and wanted to get that over and have a crack at Collier who was a more worthy opponent. McGarrity heard all this and looked as if he would like to give Mills a dead leg – or possibly a dead head.

Then it stops raining and Mr Evans the games master and Miss Sylvia Truman who is our lady games master go out and skid about on the grass courts to see if they are safe. They are not. Even then I do not realize what is going to happen because Collier comes over to the dark corner where I am skulking with my cold spotty arms and starts talking to *me*!

'Jane Turner, isn't it?' he says. He must have asked somebody because he couldn't possibly know otherwise. I was only a fourth year then.

And I say, 'Yes.'

And he says, 'I see you every day on the bus, don't I?'

And I say, 'Yes,' although I travel downstairs and he travels up, among the smokers, although of course he doesn't smoke himself because of his athlete's lungs.

And he says, 'You're an umpire today, aren't you?'

And I say, 'Yes.'

And he says, 'Do you play?'

And I say, 'Yes,' which I do and not badly but I don't go in for tournaments because people watch and if I was being watched I would foul it up.

'We have a court at home,' he says which I know because he is a near neighbour like Carson, although me and Carson live on the Glebelands Estate and the Colliers live in the Old Rectory. And then he says, '*You ought to come over and play, sometime.*'

And I can't believe this but I say, 'Yes. Yes please. Yes, I'd like that.' And I still don't believe it.

And he says, 'Bring your cousin and make up a foursome. That was your cousin who was sitting next to you, wasn't it, on the bus?' And I know he must have been asking about me because my cousin Dawn is only staying with us for a week.

And I say, 'Yes,' and he says, 'Come on Friday, then,' and I say, 'Yes.' Again. And I wonder how I can last out till Friday evening. It is only three-fifteen on Wednesday.

And then Mr Evans and Miss Sylvia Truman come in from skidding about and Mr Evans, finalist in the All-England Anthropoid Ape Championships says, 'The grass is kaput. We'll have to finish up on Centre Court. Come on Collier. Come on Mills,' and McGarrity says, 'Mills hasn't beaten me yet, Sir,' and Sir says, 'Oh, well,' and doesn't say, 'It's a foregone conclusion,' and Miss Sylvia Truman says, 'Well hurry up and finish him off, Mills,' in a voice that McGarrity isn't supposed to hear but does.

(If Miss Sylvia Truman *was* a man instead of just looking like one, McGarrity would take her apart, but doesn't, because she isn't. Also, she is much bigger than McGarrity.)

And Sir says, 'Where's the umpire?' and I say, 'I am,' and Sir says, 'Can you manage?' and I say, 'I haven't made any mistakes yet.'

'But it's the *final*,' says Fiery Fred Truman who thinks I am an imbecile – I have heard her but I say I can manage and I am desperate to do it because of Collier playing and perhaps Sir has been fortifying himself with the flat bottle he thinks we don't know about but which we can see the outline of in his hip pocket, because he says, 'All right, Jane,' and I can't believe it.

But anyway, we all go out to the damp green canyon that is Centre Court and I go up my ladder and Mills finishes off McGarrity love, love, love, love, and still I don't make any mistakes.

*Sports at School*

And then suddenly *everybody* is there to watch because it is Mills versus Collier and we all want/know that Collier will win.

Collier comes and takes off his sweater and hangs it on the rung of my chair and says, 'Don't be too hard on me, Jane,' with that smile that would make you love him even if you didn't like him, and I say, 'I've got to be impartial,' and I am afraid that I won't be impartial.

He says, 'I won't hold it against you, Jane.' And he says, 'Don't forget Friday.'

I say, 'I won't forget Friday,' as loudly as I can so that as many people as possible will hear, which they do.

You can see them being surprised all round the court.

'And don't forget your cousin,' he says, and I say, 'Oh, she's going home on Thursday morning.'

'Some other time, then,' he says.

'No, no.' I said. '*I* can come on Friday,' but he was already walking on to the court and he just looked over his shoulder and said, 'No, it doesn't matter,' and all round the court you could see people not being surprised. And I was up there on that lousy stinking bloody ladder and *everybody* could see me.

I thought I was going to cry and spent a long time putting my glasses on. Collier and Mills began to knockup and I got out the pencil and the score cards and broke the point off the pencil. I didn't have another one and I didn't want to show my face asking anybody to lend me one so I had to bite the wood away from the lead and of course it didn't have a proper point and made two lines instead of one. And gritty.

And then I remembered that I had to start them off so I said, 'Play, please. Collier to serve.' He had won the toss. Naturally.

My voice had gone woolly and my glasses had steamed over and I was sure people were laughing, even if they weren't. Then I heard this voice down by my feet saying, 'Let him get on with it. If he won't play with you on Friday he can play with himself,' which kind of remark would normally make me go red only I was red already. I looked down and there was Carson looking not at all well because of his foot, probably, but he gave me an evil wink and I remembered that he was a very kind person, really. I remembered that he sometimes gave me a glass of beer when he was baby-sitting. (I was only eleven, then, when he baby-sat. My mother was fussy about leaving us and there was my baby brother as well. He wasn't really sitting with *me*.)

So I smiled and he said, 'Watch the court, for God's sake, they've started,' and they had.

'That's a point to Collier,' he said, and I marked it down and dared not take my eyes off court after that, even to thank him. I looked down again when they changed ends and Carson had gone. (I asked him later where he had gone to and he said he went to throw up. I hope all this doesn't make Carson sound too *coarse*. He was in great pain. It turned out that he had broken a bone in his foot but we didn't know that, then. There are a lot of bones in the foot although you think of it as being solid – down to the toes, at any rate.)

Collier wasn't having it all his own way hooray hooray. Mills was very good too and the first set went to a tiebreak. I still wasn't making any mistakes. But when they came off the court after the tiebreak which Collier won, and did Wimbledony things with towels and a bit of swigging and spitting, he kept not looking at me. I mean, you could definitely see him *not* looking at me. Everybody could see him *not* looking at me; remembering what he had said about Friday and what I had said about Friday, as loudly as I could.

I was near to crying again, and what with that and the state of the official school pencil, the score card began to be in a bit of a mess and I suddenly realized that I was putting Collier's point on the wrong line. And of course, I called out, 'Advantage Mills,' when it should have been 40–30 to Collier and he yelled at me to look at what I was doing.

You don't argue with the umpire. You certainly don't *yell* at the umpire, but he did. I know I was wrong but he didn't have to yell. I kept thinking about him yelling and about Friday and in the next game I made the same mistake again and he was saying, 'That's all I need; a cross-eyed umpire. There's eight hundred

*Sports at School*

---

people in this school can't we find *one* with twenty-twenty vision?' If Fiery Fred or Orang-Evans had heard he might not have, but he was up by the net and facing away from them. He got worse and worse. Abusive.

Then Mills won the next game without any help from me and I thought, 'At least he's not having another walkover,' and I remembered what Carson had said. 'He doesn't care where he puts his feet.' And of course, after that, I couldn't help looking at his feet and Carson was right. He didn't care where he put them. He had this very fantastic service that went up about ten yards before he hit the ball, but his toes were over the base line three times out of five. I don't know why nobody noticed. I suppose they were all watching the fantastic ten-yard service and anyway, nobody looks at feet.

At first I forgot that this was anything to do with me; when I did remember I couldn't bear to do anything about it, at first. Then it was Mills who was serving and I had time to think.

I thought, 'Why should he get away with it?'

Then I thought, 'He gets away with everything,' and I realized that Carson probably hadn't been talking about real feet but feet was all I could think of.

Collier served. His feet were not where they should have been.

'Fifteen-love.'

I thought, I'll give you one more chance, because he was playing so well and I didn't want to spoil that fantastic service. But he had his chance, and he did it again. It was a beautiful shot, an ace, right down the centre line, and Mills never got near it.

I said, 'Foot fault.'

There was a sort of mumbling noise from everyone watching and Collier scowled but he had to play the second service. Mills tipped it back over the net and Collier never got near it.

'Fifteen all.'

'Foot fault.'

# Feet

He was going to argue but of course he couldn't because feet is not what he looked at when he was serving.

'Fifteen-thirty.' His second service wasn't very good, really.

'Foot fault.'

'Fifteen-forty.'

And then he did begin to look, and watching his feet he had to stop watching the ball and all sorts of things began to happen to his service.

Mills won that set.

'What the hell are you playing at, Turner?' said Collier, when they came off court and he called me a vindictive little cow while he was towelling and spitting but honestly, I never called foot fault if it wasn't one.

They went back for the third set and it was Collier's service. He glared at me like he had death-ray eyeballs and tossed up the first ball. And looked up.

And looked down at his feet.

And looked up again, but it was too late and the ball came straight down and bounced and rolled away into the crowd.

So he served again, looked up, looked down, and tried to move back and trod on his own foot and fell over.

People laughed. A laugh sounds terrible on Centre Court with all those walls to bounce off. Some of the algae had transferred itself to his shorts.

By now, *everybody* was looking at his feet.

He served a double fault.

'So who's winning?' said Alan Carson, back again and now looking greener than Collier's shorts. I knew he would understand because he *had* come back instead of going home to pass out which was what he should have been doing.

'I am,' I said, miserably.

'Two Pyrrhic victories in one afternoon?' said Alan. 'That must be some kind of a record.'

'It must be,' I said. 'It's got a hole in it.'

# Games Should Not be Compulsory

*Dorian Wood*

The education reforms of the present government have missed a golden opportunity to remove compulsory games from the curriculum: the philosophy which justified the inclusion of games in schools went out with the last copy of *The Boys' Own Paper*.

There has never been a better time to rethink fundamentally the provision of school sport. If education really is facing financial pressures, this measure would not only save money but would generate wealth.

Perhaps the Battle of Waterloo was won on the playing fields of Eton – but I doubt the feat is to be repeated. Or at least, not by the pupils of Anytown Comprehensive.

No longer does school sport laud any kind of *esprit de corps*. On the contrary, much of the sports activity in today's schools encourages an individualistic, introspective and selfish approach where winning is the only consideration.

In the past society aspired to value comradeship, a puritanical notion of gritting teeth as a way to some sort of superior state. Team games were a means of artificially creating a situation of strife where only teamwork would pull through.

Games were a proving ground for fortitude, sound values and leadership. The hero of *The Boys' Own Paper* was the chap who remained modest and 'a team man' while pulling off some heroic feat (preferably while enduring some excruciating discomfort or personal tragedy). 'Games' posed tests of nebulous, now seemingly almost sentimental ideas of comradeship, integrity and honour.

The now thrice-weekly dose of sport on television has crushed these old-fashioned notions beneath the heavy, spiked and logo-festooned boot of professionalism. Players, presumably to boost their standing with an impressionable section of the public, even abuse members of their own team for the slightest imperfection.

A schoolboy learns meanness and intolerance an an integral part of his sport.

This would be less serious if schools did not actually encourage an unsportsmanlike attitude. But many P.E. teachers have developed their interest in, or on the fringes of, professional sport. Many do not know how to lose honourably, nor teach their pupils to. They may even

## Games Should Not be Compulsory

join in abuse from the touch-line or advocate some dubious tactical ploy under the euphemism 'gamesmanship'.

Just as serious is the way that school sport has encouraged the proliferation of non-team activities, many of which are purely recreational and have little educational justification. The only interaction these participants in 'individual sports' have with other human beings is as opponents — people to be beaten in the most emphatic way.

What sort of social lesson is this? These sports are often very expensive to equip too. The capitation allowance given to sports departments is enormous and way beyond what is justified in educational terms.

This is especially true if one includes the cost of groundsman's fees and transport to away matches. School teams are invariably dominated by a small group of 'natural' players who occupy most positions in most teams. Thus a very small coterie may soak-up a massive part of school funds. Conversely, perhaps half of the other pupils would give-up games if they had the choice to do so.

Games should be offered as a voluntary option like most other subjects. With this situation it would then be consistent for games staff to encourage a ruthless approach in harmony with the realities of professional sport. The subject would have become just another vocational course with employment prospects taught alongside the actual physical activity.

With fewer pupils schools can cut back on the provision of equipment and the size of sports fields. Most sports fields are in urban areas with high land values. This premium building land could be sold-off to generate income for the other capital-intensive education activities which are at present less well funded than many P.E. departments.

However, sports departments could also benefit by having greater resources per child once the number of participants has fallen.

In this year of the Olympic Games, with its vulgar professionalism, our schools ought to take this bold step. They can then recognize the harsh professionalism of 'specialist sport' for what it is, while doing away with the hypocrisy of seeming to offer sadly outdated social and moral training.

*Sports at School*

# Miss Willis, P. E.

*Judith Nicholls*

With shorts in modest pleats,
well-pressed,
white shirt well-buttoned
(over aertex vest),
Miss Willis ruled the field.
Her hair, which longer
might have swung too wild,
lies cropped in regimented waves,
disorder unrevealed.

From light and even tan
(Miss Willis was not noted
for excess)
she summons us to heel;
in gym or hockey field
stares disbelieving
at our feckless limbs.
Refuses notes (well-forged)
for missing games or shower,
propels us with no mercy
to the high jump
or the double bar.

She fell
(if such was possible)
for some wee Scot,
a German teacher
half her size;

opted for teamwork (licensed)
and the marriage stakes –
her biggest hurdle
in our eyes.

*Sports at School*

# Caught in the Act

*Leslie Davies*

On Wednesday afternoon when the bell rang for two and a half solid hours of games, amidst the girlish laughter and the cries of 'Super' I stood waiting my chance to make a bee-line for the lavatory. Once there with a couple of soul-mates, we all got into one lavatory, locked the door and stood on the seat. This was so when the games-mistress came in searching for strayed victims she wouldn't see our feet through the gap at the bottom of the door. It always seemed an age waiting for her to come in, look around, and go out again. When she had gone we were free to do anything we liked. Sometimes we played with the costumes and make up from the dressing-up box in the attic.

One terrible day a new lighter step came into the lavatory as we stood trembling on the seat. We didn't make a sound, not knowing who it might be, then suddenly from above our heads a voice said 'What on earth are you doing?'

It was the new assistant games-mistress, young and keen and obviously destined to go far in her chosen profession. She had got on to the seat in the lavatory next to ours, hitched herself up so she could look over and was staring down at us.

We trooped out shamefacedly. When she got us to the changing-room none of us had our games-kit.

'Right,' she said. 'You'll just have to do it in your vests and knickers.'

## *Practice Makes Perfect*
# High Dive

*James Kirkup*

It feels very lonely, up here against the clouds
and girders of the glass roof. The pool so far away,
framed in flowers of a thousand upturned faces.

Walk to the brink, turn, and carefully
(firm toes gripping this last hold on life)
hang heels in space. Face a blank wall.

Raise arms slowly, sideways, shoulder-high,
silent passion, dream-deep concentration
foretelling every second of the coming flight.

Then with a sudden upward beat of palms,
of arms like wings, gathering more than thought
launch backwards into take-off, into one ball

roll for a quadruple reverse somersault
that at the last split second flicks
open like a switchblade –

feet pointed as in prayer, neat-folded hands
stab the heavens like a dagger, plunge
deep into the pool's azure flesh – without a splash.

# Practice Makes Perfect

*Daley Thompson*

People never believe me when I tell them that being a top athlete is a full-time occupation that is often every bit as boring as any 9–5 job – but it's absolutely true.

There are times during the long winter months when the monotony of that seven-days-a-week training routine really brings me down. There aren't many competitions in the winter and so it becomes that much harder to motivate yourself.

The public only see the glamorous side of it when you're racing to a glorious victory in front of a packed crowd or hitting the headlines as you break another record. What they don't see is the shivering athlete standing in the middle of the frozen wastes of Crystal Palace on a January afternoon trying to summon the enthusiasm to throw a shot that is so cold it sticks to the skin of your neck – unless you have had the foresight to ring up the groundsman in advance and get him to soak it in a bucket of hot water before you arrive.

Crystal Palace is not the most inviting place on earth even at the best of times and when there's an icy wind swirling round the stadium and the place is half waterlogged and the damp has got into the electrics and fused all the lights – well, sometimes I'd give anything to be sitting behind a desk in a nice warm office! The only way I can keep my interest up then is to remind myself that I'm too far along the line to quit now. There's nothing else I can do any more!

And, of course, trainer Bruce is always there cracking the whip behind me and making sure that I'm not slacking. Morale boosting is one of his duties. I must admit that every now and again I do play truant and sneak a day off when I should be training. The only time I can do that is when Bruce is out of town and even then I have to be careful because he is always checking up on me. He phones up every now and again just to make sure I'm where I ought to be. Occasionally we have big rows – more often than not when he has called in the morning and found me still in bed when I should be ready to start my first run of the day. We have murders then.

Most of the time Bruce and I get on pretty well although it is obviously difficult for two people to work together as closely as we do without occasionally getting on

## Practice Makes Perfect

each other's nerves. The most constant bone of contention is one which I suspect exists between a lot of athletes and their trainers — he thinks I would never have got where I am today if it weren't for him, whereas I'm cocky enough to think that I don't need him really. After all, I'm the champion — not him!

Of course, I'm being unfair. You do need somebody watching you all the time because a lot of the training involves technical rather than physical factors. Very often it takes an expert outsider to spot what you are doing wrong and how you could alter your technique slightly to achieve a better result.

The fact that I do ten events instead of one doesn't mean that I train ten times harder than other athletes. But I do probably train more consistently. The idea is not to drive myself into the ground or past the pain barrier as footballers and some middle distance and long distance runners do. The kind of all-round strength, fitness, speed, power and technique demanded of a decathlete requires a completely different kind of training programme to that followed by, for instance, my friends, Sebastian Coe and Steve Ovett. Those guys do things that make me tired just to think about them. Like running reps — repetitions — of 200 to 800 metres with just a few seconds rest in between. That's how they build up the kind of fitness and stamina that enables them to put in a sprint finish at the end of a fast 1,500 metres race. There's no point in me driving myself to that point of exhaustion every day when it's just as important for me to perfect my long jump take-off or my pole vault run-up or my javelin throwing action.

A typical winter week for me starts off with a fairly gentle twenty-minute run on Monday morning. Then in the afternoon I go down to Crystal Palace and work from 2 pm until about 7 pm on my sprinting, hurdling, long jump and high jump.

Tuesday starts with a two-mile run down to the sports centre in Crawley where I'll throw shot and javelin for an hour or so. Then I break for lunch after which I'll throw javelin and discus for an hour. Another break and then it is an hour-and-a-half of weight training — the thing I detest most because it's both boring and tiring.

Wednesday is my really big day. It starts with a two-mile run down to the sports centre and then into an hour or so of throwing. I start with the shot and the routine is always the same. Ten minutes is spent warming up, then I'll throw perhaps twenty times concentrating on different parts of the technique, and I'll end up throwing six times flat out. I repeat much the same sequences with the discus.

*Practice Makes Perfect*

---

After lunch I have another run and a further hour of throwing and then at about 3.30 pm I drive to Crystal Palace for a three-hour session of running, jumping, vaulting and hurdling. In each case the sequence is much the same – ten to fifteen minutes of warm up followed by practice jumps, vaults or hurdles, when I focus on aspects of technique, followed by ten or twelve full-out attempts.

Thursday is a repeat of Tuesday's programme and on Friday the morning and afternoon are spent throwing and running down at the Crawley sports centre before going up to Crystal Palace in the evening for a session of circuit training.

Saturday and Sunday afternoons are both spent at Crystal Palace on a general programme of running and jumping.

This weekly routine is not rigidly strict and obviously I can vary it every now and again to take in other commitments. But if I do miss a day I tend to work much harder the next day. And I cannot afford to break the routine too often or it does begin to tell on me.

I mustn't paint too gloomy a picture of the drudgery of training. It is only fair to confess that at the end of February each year I take off to California for a couple of months to train in the sunshine of San Diego. I really enjoy myself there although I still work hard. I actually get out of bed at 7 am – which is amazing for me – so that I can get in a good session before the sun gets too hot. And then I have a second session late in the afternoon. It makes a great change from Crystal Palace and it sets me up nicely for the season.

The season starts back home in May, and from then until September my weekly routine is different because there are so many competitions. Apart from the Internationals and major meetings I turn out anything up to three times a week for my club Essex Beagles. I love competing and it doesn't bother me at all that some of the meetings are very small affairs.

Obviously I don't do the decathlon at this level – I just go in for the individual events. I usually take part in the 100 metres, the shot, the discus, the high jump and the pole vault. The greatest number of events I have ever done at one meeting is seven. Even at this local level the standard is very high, and in most cases I'll find myself competing against people who are a little better than me in their particular sport – particularly the throwing events where I am weaker and don't really figure in the top ten national ratings. So I rarely find myself in the situation of having a walkover.

# A Life in the Day of Joanne Conway

*Jenny Woolf*

**Joanne Conway is Britain's top woman figure skater, and is due to compete in the European figure skating championships which start in Birmingham on Tuesday. She won her fourth successive British title last November. She grew up in North Shields with her mother Miriam, a nurse, father Tom, a sheet metal worker, and brother and sister Adrian, 22, and Lesley, 24. After three years' training in Colorado Springs, she now lives in California, where she is trained by Robin Cousins.**

I came to live in America three years ago when I was 14, and I spend only two months of the year in England now. Before I went away I used to get up at 4.30, go to the rink, go back to the rink at lunchtime, then at teatime after school. I'd come back at about eight o'clock and try to do my homework. But I couldn't cope with it.

Here in California I'll get up around 7.30 and have bran flakes, corn flakes or eggs, and herbal tea. Then I drive to the rink – I've got my own car – and skate for three hours.

I live in the Ice Castle Training Camp up in the mountains at Lake Arrowhead. It's like a motel, and it's great. It holds about 50 people, eight to a room, with bunk beds, and we have lots of fun.

They run summer schools at the camp, and sometimes it's packed out, but I'm the only person of my age who lives here permanently. I can do more or less what I like . . . Well, I let the houseparents know what I'm doing, but they don't argue with me about it.

I love the facilities we have; they're just incredible. We have a restaurant, a weight training room, swimming pool, Jacuzzi, hot tub, two dance rooms, an open-air rink, and they're building a training rink with heating.

The training sessions are 45 minutes long. I usually do three freestyles – that's skating, jumps, spins: the stuff you see on TV – and two figure patches: the technical practice. Robin Cousins, my coach, gives me two or three lessons a day, sometimes more. They're often not so much lessons as talking about things like programmes and music and costumes. My mam used to do my costumes, but now she sends ideas and I get them made up.

*Practice Makes Perfect*

Mam loved sport when she was young. So does my brother – he's football crazy – and my dad's keen on darts. My sister's idea of sport is to sit on the couch and read 10 books. My sister and brother took me on the ice rink for the first time when I was about four. When I was little I did riding, roller-skating, diving, ballroom dancing, ballet, jazz, tap. I was in the netball team and the north-east gymnastic squad, too; I had to choose between that and skating.

I gave up school when I went to America. I thought, I won't get another crack at the skating, but I can take up my education again any time. Anyway, my brother's got O and A levels and he was out of work. You cannot get jobs in the north-east, so you think what's the use of qualifications?

After the morning session I go back and have lunch. I'll probably have a baked potato and salad and, very rarely, yoghurt. I go back to the rink about one o'clock and skate for another two hours.

Then I do my messages – that's phone calls, errands – and have my evening meal. I'm vegetarian and I always have pasta. I've got a thing about pasta. Then I do weight training till maybe nine o'clock.

I couldn't get these facilities in England. English rinks need to make money so they have public skating and ice hockey which mess up the ice. They even do pop concerts, when they board the ice over for a fortnight. How can figure skaters train properly?

I love England and seeing my family but I may settle in America. Or I may not. I'm too young to say. I'm not very concerned about making money, but here I could make thousands; in England I'd make hundreds.

If I do make a lot of money I'd like to have my own rink in the north-east and let talented young figure skaters use it free. Or manage a rink. When I turn professional I'd like to teach the children of Whitley Bay. I've always wanted to teach; I love children. There are some children living at the camp, eight years and younger. I couldn't have handled it when I was that age and some of them cannot handle themselves either. I'm like their big sister. They come to me with their problems, ask me to go to the shops for them, and I do.

I'm exhausted after weight training, but it's a laugh because we all do it together. Then after, if it's nice, we'll sit in the hot tub and have a Jacuzzi. It's outside and its great sitting in the snow with all the steam, gossiping about anything and everything . . . *except* skating. Mostly about men. Skaters are usually man-crazy because they only ever associate with other female skaters.

## A Life in the Day of Joanne Conway

At weekends we go on outings: Disneyland or shopping malls or beaches. Nightlife in LA is terrible. You've got to be over 21 and there aren't any pubs. I don't have a boyfriend. If I could have one I would, but there's just nobody to meet in the camp. In the winter, even though it's warm in LA, you need snow-chains to get up the mountain road. Some boys who live in LA might be prepared to drive up here, but not many.

I've made sacrifices. Friends, boys, clubs, discos. It does bother me, and yet it doesn't, you know. Because skating is what I'm here for and that's what I'm going to do.

I appreciate the sacrifices my family's made too. I'm sponsored by C & A now, but before that my parents paid £100 a week, and they don't have lots of money. And I know my brother and sister have done without things to pay for what I need. I've often thought: should I take all this money? It's always money into *me*. It's a responsibility ... Then I think, well, if they didn't want to, they wouldn't have done it.

On Tuesdays I see my sports psychologist, Linda. She's helped me a lot. My mam thinks it is a pity the media expected me to get a medal as soon as I became known. I can do the jumps; it's just getting the confidence back to do them in competition and in the public eye. I know I'm better now than I ever was. But the press and television in skating, they just try to knock people all the time. Like the one girl that fell down recently – she was second in Great Britain – and OK she fell, but why tell the world she did so badly? She was still second.

Linda can't do magic but if I fall on the ice or do something wrong I can talk about why I did it, which helps me understand how not to do it again. At one time I wanted to succeed so badly and I was pushing myself so hard that things weren't working so well. The idea Linda put into my head was: say I was looking for a boyfriend and wanted one so very, very badly, then he'd probably never come. But if I could be more relaxed and say, 'Oh, well, I'll get one sometime,' then he might knock at the door next day. She made me see that sometimes you have to wait for things to come to you.

I have a one-channel mind. My dad always told me to think about where I want to end up, forget about what's in between, and everything else is a bonus. Aim at where I want to get. And I do. In five years' time I want to be World, European and Olympic champion, I want to be the best. I've worked hard and I think I deserve it.

I don't think I could do all this training if I lived at home with my family. That's why I don't want them out here. I'd have too much of

*Practice Makes Perfect*

a good time. I'd be lazing round in the day, living it up all night.

In fact, I'm a real night person. I'm ready to start my day at 10 o'clock at night. But by 10 o'clock in America I just fall into bed. I'm exhausted, I'm dead; absolutely dead.

# Lean Lesson

*Matthew Bridgeman*

Matthew Bridgeman used to be a tubby 12-year-old. Now he's a lightweight teenager who's becoming more successful with his running thanks to following a sensible schedule and diet.

---

Training Schedule
MONDAY: 10 × 100 metre uphill sprints; with one mile warm up and down.
TUESDAY: 2 miles fast. (Done in about 9 mins 40 sec)
WEDNESDAY: 5 miles steady. (Done in about 30 mins)
THURSDAY: REST
FRIDAY: 10 × 200 metre sprints; with 200 metre jog recovery
SATURDAY: 3.5 mile cross-country.
SUNDAY: 4 × 600 metre sprints; with 600 metre jog recovery.
Plus very light weight-training every day except Thursday.

---

A little less than a year ago I was a tubby 12-year-old, feeding on chips and chocolate bars. My idea of exercise was changing TV channels by remote control. Now I am a lean 13-year-old who eats baked potatoes and natural crunch bars, with a regular training schedule.

One day I found myself glued to the 'box' watching an international athletics meeting at Gateshead. It looked so much fun. All those strong athletes coasting round a 400 metre track at high speed. So, I thought I would have a go at it. The next day was warm and sunny with just a little light breeze. I donned my tracksuit bottoms, school athletics vest and best trainers, and I set off on a one mile run. It was not as bad as I thought it was going to be and it took me just under eight minutes.

The next day was a different matter. I was as stiff as a board and I could hardly kneel down! But I went out again. And again and again. The stiffness went away and I did nothing but improve. After about two weeks I started doing two miles every day. Then 2.5 miles, and 3 miles, gradually building up my stamina.

I decided to cut out all that excess sugar and fat from my diet. It didn't feel like 'slimming' because I wasn't eating less, just eating differently. I became a 'health-fooder'. Porridge oats for breakfast, wholemeal bread in my lunch-box, chilli beans for dinner. It all seemed very filling! I drank just as much milk as before, only now it was skimmed milk. And I ate fresh fruit and yoghurt instead of cakes and puddings. Already, I was feeling fitter and looking better.

Three and a half months after I

*Practice Makes Perfect*

---

started training I had a talk with one of my dad's friends who was a running coach. He told me that my training was lacking two factors: SPEED and STRENGTH. Also, the fact that I didn't have any rest days wasn't good for me or for my running. He gave me a training programme which I have basically followed ever since.

My schedule has changed a lot since the early days when every day was a 2.5 mile run. The times have changed a lot too. I would have taken about 17 minutes to get round that 2.5 mile circuit then. Now it would take me under 12.30.

Just after Christmas, to strengthen my arms and legs, and for more sprinting power, I took up light weight-training using dumb-bells. I've read a lot of articles which claim that weight-training is bad for your body if your body is still growing. But I think that if you are pretty fit, and do not use too heavy weights, it will help your running a lot. I never lift anything over 20 kgs at any one time. Then, at half-term, I got a weight-bench and bar-bell. The weight-bench has leg-extension attachments, and the use of these in my training has really put muscles onto my legs.

My running has had its good and bad days, sad and funny days. There was the day I ran off the road onto the beach to find that the tide had come in. It was a very high tide. I had to run knee-deep in water for over two miles! I remember one particularly bad day when I did a cross-country run in deep snow and I seemed to be more on my bum than on my feet. That experience taught me not to run in deep snow again.

The obsession called 'NOT MISSING TRAINING' can be dangerous! Sad days are when you get sick or injured and cannot run. This winter I had a chest cold which stopped my training for a whole week! But every runner has good days. These are the days when everything goes right, you feel great, and you set a personal best; like last Wednesday, when I ran 38.30 for my five mile training run in the rain.

A recent contributor to *Today's Runner* considered that it was helpful to have some target to attain. So, I hope to see you at the 1996 Olympics!

# Boxer Man In-a Skippin Workout

*James Berry*

Skip on big man, steady steady.
Giant, skip-dance easy easy!
Braad and tall a-work shaped limbs,
a-move sleek self wid style well trimmed.
Gi ryddm yu ease of being strang.
Movement is a meanin and a song.
   Tek yu lickle trips in yu skips, man.
   Be dat dancer-runner man.

Yu so easy easy. Go-on na big man!
Fighta man is a ryddm man
full of de go, free free.
Movement is a dream and a spree.
Yu slow down, yu go faas.
Sweat come oil yu body like race horse.
   Tek yu lickle trips in yu skips, man.
   Be dat dancer-runner man – big man!

# *Track and Field*

# To James

*Frank Horne*

Do you remember
How you won
That last race?
How you flung your body
At the start . . .
How your spikes
Ripped the cinders
In the stretch . . .
How you catapulted
Through the tape . . .
Do you remember?
Don't you think
I lurched with you
Out of those starting holes?
Don't you think
My sinews tightened
At those first
Few strides . . .
And when you flew into the stretch
Was not all my thrill
Of a thousand races
In your blood?
At your final drive
Through the finish line
Did not my shout

Tell of the
Triumphant ecstasy
Of victory?
Live
As I have taught you
To run, Boy —
It's a short dash
Dig your starting holes
Deep and firm
Lurch out of them
Into the straightaway
With all the power
That is in you
Look straight ahead
To the finish line
Think only of the goal
Run straight
Run high
Run hard
Save nothing
And finish
With an ecstatic burst
That carries you
Hurtling
Through the tape
To victory . . .

# Raymond's Run

*Toni Cade Bambara*

I don't have much work to do around the house like some girls. My mother does that. And I don't have to earn my pocket money by running errands and selling Christmas cards. My brother George does that. And anything else that's got to get done, my father does.

All I have to do is mind my brother Raymond, which is enough. He's much bigger and he's older, too, but a lot of people call him my little brother because he's not quite right and needs looking after. And if any of these smart mouths try to pick on Raymond, they have to deal with me, and I don't believe in just standing around talking. I'd much rather knock them down and take my chances, even if I am a girl with skinny arms and a squeaky voice, which is how I got my nickname Squeaky. And if things get too tough, I run.

As anybody can tell you, I'm the fastest thing on two feet. There is no track meet where I don't win the first-place medal. I used to win the 20-yard dash when I was a little kid. Nowadays it's the 100-yard dash.

I'm the swiftest thing in the neighbourhood. Everybody knows that except the two people who know better – my father and me. My father can beat me in a race to Amsterdam Avenue with me getting a head start and him running with his hands in his pocket and whistling. But can you imagine a thirty-five year-old man stuffing himself into a pair of shorts just to beat his kid in a race?

So, as far as everyone's concerned, I'm the fastest. Except for Gretchen, who has put out the story that she is going to win the first-place medal this year. Ridiculous. No one can beat me, and that's all there is to that.

After school I usually take a walk down Broadway so I can practice my breathing exercises. I always keep Raymond walking

*Track and Field*

on the inside, close to the buildings, because he's subject to fits of fantasy and sometimes starts thinking he's a circus performer and that the curb is a tightrope strung high in the air.

Or sometimes, if I don't watch him, he'll run across traffic to one of the parks and give the pigeons a fit. Then I have to go around apologizing to all the people sitting on the benches who are all shook up with the pigeons fluttering around them, scattering newspapers and upsetting their sack lunches.

So I keep Raymond on the inside, and today he starts playing like he's driving a stagecoach. This is OK with me so long as he doesn't run over me or interrupt my breathing exercises, which I have to do on account of I'm serious about my running and don't care who knows it.

Now some people like to act like things come easy to them and won't let on that they practise. But not me. You can see me any time of the day practising. I never walk if I can run, and Raymond always keeps up because if he hangs back, someone is likely to walk up behind him and get smart and take his allowance.

So I'm going down Broadway breathing out and breathing in, in counts of seven. And suddenly here comes Gretchen with her sidekicks – Mary Louise, who used to be a friend of mine when she first moved to Harlem from Cincinnati, and Rosie, who is as fat as I am skinny and has a big mouth where Raymond is concerned and is too stupid to know that there is not a big deal of difference between herself and Raymond.

So they are coming up Broadway, and I see right away that it's going to mean trouble because the street ain't that big. First I think I'll step into the candy store and look over the new comics and let them pass. But that's chicken, and I've got a reputation to consider. So then I think I'll just walk straight on through them, or over them if necessary. But as they get to me, they slow down.

'You signing up for the Field Day races?' smiles Mary Louise.

A dumb question like that doesn't deserve an answer.

'I don't think you're going to win this time,' says Rosie, trying to signify with her hands on her hips all salty.

# Raymond's Run

'I always win 'cause I'm the best,' I say straight at Gretchen.

Gretchen smiles. But it's not really a smile, and I'm thinking that girls never ever really smile at each other because they don't know how and don't want to know how.

Then Rosie looks at Raymond, who has just brought his make-believe stagecoach to a stop. And she's about to see what trouble she can stir up through him. 'What grade you in now, Raymond?' she asks.

'You got anything to say to my brother, you say it to me,' I tell her.

'What are you, his mother?' sasses Rosie.

'That's right, fatso.'

So they just stand there, and Gretchen puts her hands on her hips and is about to say something but doesn't. Then she walks around me and looks me up and down, but she keeps moving up Broadway and her sidekicks follow her. So me and Raymond smile at each other and he says 'Giddyap' to his team of horses and I continue with my breathing exercises.

On Field Day I take my time getting to the park because the track meet is the last thing on the programme. I put Raymond in the swings. Then I look around for Mr Pearson who pins the numbers on. I'm really looking for Gretchen, if you want to know the truth, but she's not around.

The park is packed with parents in hats and little kids in white dresses and light blue suits. Some older guys with their caps on backwards are leaning against the fence swirling basketballs on the tips of their fingers, waiting for all these crazy people to clear out so they can play.

Then here comes Mr Pearson with his clipboard and his cards and pencils and whistles and fifty million other things he's always dropping. He sticks out in a crowd because he looks like he's on stilts. We used to call him Jack the Beanstalk to get him mad. But I'm the only one who can outrun him and get away, and now I'm too grown for silly name-calling.

'Well, Squeaky,' he says, checking my name off the list and handing me number seven and two pins.

*Track and Field*

I'm thinking he's got no right to call me Squeaky if I don't call him Beanstalk. 'Hazel Elizabeth Deborah Parker,' I correct him, and tell him to write it down that way on his board.

'Well, Hazel Elizabeth Deborah Parker, are you going to give someone else a break this year?'

I squint at him real hard to see if he is seriously thinking I should lose the race on purpose just to give someone else a break.

'Only eight girls running this time,' he continues, shaking his head sadly like it's my fault all of New York didn't turn out in sneakers. 'That new girl should give you a run for your money.' He looks around the park for Gretchen like a periscope in a submarine movie. 'Wouldn't it be a nice gesture if you were to . . . to ahh . . .'

I give him such a look that he can't finish putting that idea into words. Then I pin number seven on myself and stomp away. I'm so burnt. I go straight to the track and stretch out on the grass.

The man on the loudspeaker begins calling everyone over to the track for the first event, which is the 20-yard dash. The race takes two minutes because most of the little kids don't know better than to run off the track or run the wrong way or run smack into the fence and fall down and cry.

Then comes the 50-yard dash, and I don't even bother to turn my head to watch because Raphael Perez always wins by psyching out the other runners, telling them they're going to fall on their faces or lose their shorts or something.

Then I hear my brother Raymond hollering from the swings. He knows I'm about to do my thing because the man on the loudspeaker has just announced the 100-yard dash.

I get up and slip off my sweat pants and then I see Gretchen standing at the starting line, kicking her legs like a pro. Then as I get into place, I see Raymond on the other side of the fence, bending down with his fingers on the ground just like he knew what he was doing. I start to yell at him but I don't. It burns up your energy to holler.

Just before I take off in a race, I always feel like I'm in a dream, the kind of dream you have when you're sick with fever and feel all hot and weightless. I dream I'm flying over a sandy beach in the early morning sun, touching the leaves of the trees as I fly by. And all the time I feel myself getting lighter and lighter.

Then I spread my fingers in the dirt and crouch over for the Get-On-Your-Mark yell. I stop dreaming and I am solid again and telling myself, 'Squeaky you must win. You must win. You are the fastest thing in the world. You can even beat your father if you try.'

And then I feel my weight coming back just behind my knees, then down to my feet, and the pistol shot explodes in my blood and I am off and weightless again, flying past the other runners. My arms pump up and down, and the whole world is quiet except for the crunch-crunch as I zoom over the gravel on the track.

I glance to my left, and there is no one. But to my right is Gretchen, who's got her chin jutting out as if it would win the race all by itself. And on the other side of the fence is my brother Raymond with his arms down at his side and the palms tucked up behind him, running in his very own style. It's the first time I've ever seen him do that, and I almost stop to watch.

But the white ribbon is bouncing toward me, and I tear past it, running hard till my feet – with a mind of their own – start digging up footfuls of dirt and stop me. Then all the kids standing on the sidelines pile on me, slapping me on the back with their Field Day programmes because they think I've won again and everybody on the 151st Street can walk tall for another year.

'In first place – ' The man on the loudspeaker pauses, and the loudspeaker starts to whine. Then some static. I lean down to catch my breath, and I see Gretchen doing the same thing – huffing and puffing with her hands on her hips, taking it slow, breathing in steady time like a real pro – and I sort of like her a little for the first time.

'In first place – ' Then three or four voices get all mixed up on

*Track and Field*

the loudspeaker and I dig my sneakers in the grass and stare at Gretchen who's staring back, both wondering just who did win. I can hear old Beanstalk arguing with the man on the loudspeaker about what the stop watches say.

Then I hear Raymond yanking at the fence and calling me, and I wave to shush him. But he keeps rattling the fence and then starts climbing nice and easy. And it occurs to me, watching how smoothly he climbs and remembering how he looked running with the wind pulling his mouth back and his teeth showing and all, it occurs to me that Raymond would make a very fine runner. Doesn't he always keep up with me on my practices? And he surely knows how to breathe in counts of seven 'cause he's always doing it at the dinner table.

And I'm smiling to beat the band because if I've lost this race, or if me and Gretchen have tied, or even if I've won, I can always retire as a runner and begin a whole new career as a coach with Raymond as my champion.

So I stand there laughing out loud as Raymond jumps down from the fence and runs over to me with his arms down at his side in his own running style. And by the time he comes over, I'm jumping up and down I'm so glad to see him.

But of course everyone thinks I'm jumping up and down because the men have finally gotten themselves together and the loudspeaker is announcing, 'In first place – Miss Hazel Elizabeth Deborah Parker. In second place – Miss Gretchen B. Lewis.'

And I look over at Gretchen wondering what the B. stands for. And I smile. Maybe she'd like to help me coach Raymond because she's obviously serious about running. And she nods to congratulate me. Then she smiles, too, and it's about as real a smile as girls can do for each other, considering we don't practise it as much as we should every day.

# Hero

*Mick Gowar*

'Of course I took the drugs. Look, son,
there's no fair play, no gentlemen,
no amateurs, just winning.
How old are you? Fifteen? Well,
you should know that
no one runs for fun – well, not beyond
the schoolboy stuff – eleven or twelve years old.
I'd been a pro for years;
my job – to get that Gold.

Mind you, we English are an odd lot:
like to believe we love the slob that fails,
the gentlemanly third; so any gap-toothed yob who
                                  gets the glory
also gets some gentlemanly trait: helps cripples get across
the street, nice to small animals. You know the kind of thing,
it helps the public feel it's
all legit; that sportsmanship is real and that
it's all clean fun –
the strongest, bravest, fittest
best man won.

Yeah, Steroids . . . Who do *you* think? . . .
   Oh, don't be wet –
My coach, of course, he used to get them
through this vet . . . The side effects? Well, not so bad
as these things go – for eighteen months or so

*Track and Field*

I didn't have much use for girls. But, by then I
                                      was training
for the Big One – got to keep the body pure,
not waste an ounce of effort.'

He gives a great guffaw.
A chain of spittle
rattles down the front of
his pyjama jacket.
He wipes his mouth;
His eyes don't laugh at all.

'. . . Do it again? Of course I would –
I'd cheat, I'd box, I'd spike, I'd pay the devil's price
to be that good again
for just one day. You see, at twenty-three
I peaked – got all I ever wanted:
all anyone would ever want from me.
After the race, this interviewer told me
Fifty million people's hopes and dreams had been
fulfilled – a Gold!
How many ever get that chance? I did.
Would you say No to that?
Of course not.

Damn, the bell. You'd better go, they're pretty strict.
Yeah, leave the flowers there on the top,
the nurse'll get some water and a vase.'

# The High Jump Competition
*Peter Carter*

Erika Nordern is fifteen, a gifted high jumper, who lives in East Berlin. She is taking part in the Indoor Athletics Championships and, if she wins, she will be offered a place in a special sports school with the prospect of a glittering future. Her chief rival is a girl called Karen Bloxen, who is reputed to have said that she plans to make a fool of Erika at the championships.

The rules of the competition were simple. Each girl had three attempts at the same height. Three failures at any height spelled O. U. T. but one clearance in any of the three attempts meant that the girl could go through to the next round. If the competition was a tie, that is if more than one girl went through to the final height and all failed, then the girl with the least failures overall was the winner, which meant, of course, that first, or even second time clearances could be of crucial importance.

The starting jump, at 1 metre 50 centimetres, was a relatively easy height for a goodish competition and the first girl to jump, stocky and small for a high-jumper, cleared the bar easily, as was to be expected, and so did all the others except Karen Bloxen, who chose not to jump.

So, Erika thought, it was as Fräulein Silber and herself had discussed earlier: pass a jump and put a little psychological pressure on the other competitors. For a moment she was tempted to pass herself but, she reasoned, if she did jump then the pressure would be reversed. If it came to a tie then her jump would count in her favour and Bloxen's pass would count against *her*. She wished that Fräulein Silber was there to give her advice, but as she was not, it was up to herself. Play safe, she thought, be prudent, and walked to her mark, acutely aware of the audience,

*Track and Field*

the judges, the other girls, and even more aware that she had exactly ninety seconds in which to prepare herself.

She took a deep breath, rocked forward on to her left foot and raised her hands, nodding her head as she counted her run-up, visualizing the jump. Seven metres away the crossbar set its challenge, on the track behind it runners poured past, somewhere a starting-pistol cracked. . . .

'Oh dear,' Erika murmured and, forgetting everything that she had ever learned, dashed forward like a startled pony – and brought the bar down.

Sweat glistening on her face, Erika draped her track suit around her shoulders as the judges rearranged the bar. 'That was nothing,' she told herself, 'nothing at all. Just a nervous start,' and she had two more jumps to go anyway.

Not daring to look across the track at her family, or anyone else, she waited as the bar was replaced, measured, and her number held up again.

The bar, which on her first jump had looked almost contemptibly low, now looked as high as the Television Tower; impossible for her to jump over, utterly and completely impossible, hardly worth the effort of trying, although, of course, she had to.

'Concentrate,' she said. 'Concentrate and take your time,' and doing neither she ran, missed her approach, almost took off on the wrong foot and launched herself too soon and despairingly upward. She did not turn properly and her shoulder brushed the bar. She arched her back despairingly, kicked her heels high, and bounced on the landing bed as the bar actually trembled above her. Trembled but stayed where it was.

Erika rolled off the bed unable to believe her eyes when she saw the bar still on its uprights. She was still looking at it over her shoulder as she walked back to her chair. The stocky girl grinned sympathetically, a gawky girl gave her a friendly nod, one or two of the other girls came up to her with soothing remarks and friendly advice, but Karen Bloxen turned her contemptuous head away.

## The High Jump Competition

Her track suit on, Erika slumped in her chair feeling that she deserved the contempt. A failure and a near failure at 1.50. A height she could jump with a sack of potatoes on her back. It was incredible, quite incredible. She stared at her toes, utterly dejected. 'I'll never make it,' she thought, 'never. And what will my family think? And the school and Fräulein Silber? I shall be a laughing-stock. And Herr Wolf, what will it mean to him? Nothing. A shrug of his shoulders and another girl who could not make it under pressure written off. . . . '

The second round was about to begin. The bar was edged up three centimetres and the stocky girl took her mark. With an audible grunt she cleared the bar, as did all the others except Bloxen who passed again, showing her intention with a dismissive wave of her hand.

Then Erika's number was held up. To murmurs of 'good luck' she went to her mark, made a bold effort to look confident, took her time, ran, jumped, and failed.

Unable to believe what was happening to her she trudged back to her chair, her eyes downcast. 'But I *can* do it,' she muttered as the bar was replaced. 'I can!' Although she felt in her heart that she couldn't – and she didn't, catching the bar with her heel as she turned over it.

No cheers from the Norderns, no rowdy applause from the Egon Schultz School, and an embarrassed silence from the other competitors as the bar was replaced for the second time and Erika was called for her jump.

'It is those wasted months,' she thought, as she tried to compose herself. 'All that time missed, a lack of competition.' But neither of those reasons helped her as she looked at the bar and realized that this was her last chance. If she failed now then she was out. She rocked and raised her hands, trying to allow those drilled, automatic movements to calm her. And then she ran in and in her first two strides thought of Frau Milch's comment that her run might be too narrow, tried to widen it, missed all her marks, and came into the jump with her shoulder down and her head tilted, but despite that she cleared – just.

*Track and Field*

*Just*, but as she walked back to her chair to a little muted applause from her supporters, and as she wiped the sweat from her face, at the back of her mind a tiny, tentative whisper murmured, 'You are still in, Erika, still in. You did everything wrong that a high-jumper could conceivably do but you cleared the bar – and you are still in.'

But as the third round began, out of eight girls who had started, eight girls were still in, and only Erika had failed any jump, and she had failed three times, a dismal thought to mull over as the bar went up three centimetres to 1.56. Not a sensational height by any means but tough enough to be testing, and Erika hoped fervently that it would test her opponents more than it would test herself.

It certainly tested the stocky girl, who failed, and another, spotty girl, but also Erika who, realizing on her last stride that she was too near the bar tried to pull away but was judged to have let her hand cross under the bar and so was penalized.

The stocky girl joined Erika as she sat down. 'Cheer up,' she said.

Erika adjusted her headband. 'Not much to be cheerful about, failing at these heights.'

'It's just nerves,' the stocky girl said. 'Anyone can see that you're a good jumper. Try and relax.'

'Relax!' Erika looked curiously at the girl. 'Aren't you depressed?'

'No.' The girl grinned. 'Actually, if I clear this height I'll have broken my own record.'

'What!' Erika was amazed. '1.56?'

'That's right.' The girl borrowed Erika's towel and rubbed her head vigorously.

'I'm not a high-jumper at all. Actually I'm a pentathlete – and this is my worst event! They only stuck me in because all our high-jumpers have the flu. Still, give it a go, hey?'

Yes, Erika liked that thought. Give it a go. Give it all you've got so that you could at least walk out of the arena with your

## The High Jump Competition

head held high. That was the way to do it. 'Good luck,' she said. And she meant it.

And luck – and spirit – were with the girl as she ran in, her short legs pumping away, driving forward and clearing the bar and bouncing off the landing bed with an ecstatic grin, and waving at *her* family who waved back and cheered as though she had won an Olympic Gold Medal.

But there was no luck for the spotty girl who fouled and walked back biting her lip as Erika took her mark, and cheered by the stocky girl's success, and thinking, 'If she can do it, I can,' did do it, and did it quite well she thought, as the spotty girl failed for the third time and walked off crying, her hands over her face, the first casualty of the competition. And for the first time that afternoon it occurred to Erika that other girls had their own honour to consider, and their own ambitions, and that, in his spacious office, over coffee, Herr Wolf might well have spoken to other girls as he had to her, smiling his frank, open smile, and suggesting all sorts of glorious prospects, if only....

The arc lamps shone down on an apparently endless stream of runners charging around the track, shouts and bellows echoed across the stadium, screams of excitement arose as something extraordinary happened in the Boys' Long Jump; but none of that mattered to the seven girls watching the bar being raised to 1.59 as the fourth round began.

The stocky girl failed on her first jump, as did the next girl. A platinum blonde girl went over the bar without too much trouble, so did the rather gawky girl, but number five failed ... and then Karen Bloxen stood up and joined the competition.

Was it her imagination, Erika wondered, or had the arena hushed as Bloxen, tall, elegant and aloof, walked to her mark? Certainly, and almost ludicrously she herself held her breath for a moment as Bloxen stood poised, one elegant hand held forward, the gesture itself seeming enough to hush the world if need be, and her slender white neck preordained to bear a gold medal.

*Track and Field*

'The winner,' Erika thought. 'The winner. Destined for victory. Destined for the laurel wreath.' And despite herself, but with the true, selfless admiration of one athlete for another, she felt a prickle of admiring envy as, with impeccable timing, and truly beautiful movement, Bloxen ran to the bar and jumped – floated – over it.

And that was that, Erika thought. Yes, that was that. The winner had jumped. All that remained was a battle for a place. But, still thinking too of the stocky girl's remark, she said to herself, 'Well, give it a go,' and took her mark, ran, jumped and cleared with a fine supple leap, her first really good jump. The stocky girl failed again, the other girls succeeded. The stocky girl failed for the third time but bounced away with a broad smile and a cheery wave of her hand and getting warm applause for it.

Six girls left from eight, sweating as the bar went up to 1.62. The judge raised a card, number two, and number two went to her mark, ran, jumped and failed, and failed badly. It was clear that the height was a little too much for her, and, although the platinum blonde and the gawky girl cleared, number five failed, too. With her air of supreme confidence, as if her mind were on other, and more important, affairs, Bloxen made light of her jump, and Erika, although making heavy weather of it, scraped over; another first time clearance for her, and she sat a little straighter in her chair as number two and number five tried twice more, and failed twice more, and walked off into the dark tunnel which led to the locker-room, and athletic oblivion.

And now there were only four girls left and, as the bar went up to 1 metre 65, Erika changed her socks and drank glucose and reflected on the height and the other girls. 1.65 was a reasonable challenge but not one which would have frightened her in the gym and, although she was jumping badly, unbelievably so, really, it was a height she could jump; the question was, could the other girls do it, too? No doubt they could, that was why they were in the competition, but if she could pull herself together anything might happen. She might make third place – perhaps – and then, if not Leipzig, she could probably get a place at

## The High Jump Competition

another sports school, and she would be happy enough with that.

And so Erika tried to relax as the Blonde jumped and failed. The Gawk cleared, although not without effort. Bloxen was smoothly successful but Erika lost her rhythm, although as she swerved from the bar she managed to avoid fouling. But the false try disturbed her a little and she failed on her retry. The Blonde failed again but, gritting her teeth, Erika scraped over and sat down with a prickle of excitement. If the Blonde failed again then, whatever happened, she herself was in the last three, and even if she did go out then it would not be with ignominy. But she did not think that she would go out. High-jumpers tended to get worse as a competition went on: they tired and lost their rhythm and concentration. That had happened to the girls who had been knocked out. But she felt that she was improving, not that she could possibly have got worse, and her last jump had not been that bad. She had, at last, hit all her marks accurately and she had gained real speed as she reached her take-off, and that was very important indeed.

'It's all a matter of confidence,' she muttered. 'Confidence.' Although hers was a little dented as the Blonde succeeded on her third jump.

The judges went into their ritual and Erika looked along the row of chairs with their four vacant places. At the end, Bloxen was deep in conversation with the Blonde, gesticulating and swinging her torso. Erika frowned. Clearly Bloxen was giving advice and encouragement, and of course – Erika clicked her fingers – there were only four girls left and Bloxen was trying to make sure that the Blonde was amongst the last three, thus cutting out Erika Nordern of the Egon Schultz School.

So, Erika nodded. That was the way it was going to be. Very well, she would show them. They were in for a fight such as they had never been in before, and would probably never be in again, come to that.

And then the Blonde was called for the first jump in the seventh round with the bar at 1.68.

Whatever advice Bloxen had given the Blonde it was

ineffective and, Erika thought, if the world champion herself had been advising her it would not have made any difference. The Blonde had reached her limit in the previous round and she was not going to exceed it. And then the Gawk jumped and she failed too, and although Bloxen cleared, watching her like a hawk Erika wondered if she had not been forced to stretch just a little.

With renewed hope, and with her jaw set, Erika went to her mark. For the first time that afternoon the bar looked accessible to a human being instead of a kangaroo. 'So, clear first time,' she told herself. 'Go over and put the pressure on the Blonde and the Gawk. *Do it.*'

She went through *her* ritual, gave herself every second of her ninety, made a good approach run, took off well, and clipped the bar with her heel.

As she rolled off the landing bed she groaned with frustration, but back on her chair she did not feel the despondency of the previous failures. Almost unknown to her the competition had hardened her, the blows of failure hammering out any weakness of will she might have had, as the blows of the smith drive out the impurities of iron. *Now* she could think that one jump failed meant two jumps left, and she had only barely clipped the bar with her heel. In fact she had done everything right, and felt that she had plenty of strength left, and the level of her leg could be dealt with.

She drank glucose as the blonde girl jumped again, and failed again. The Gawk jumped and cleared and Erika jumped and cleared, too, and, she thought, stylishly, and so, trying to look unconcerned, she leaned back in her chair as the Blonde took her mark.

Sweat streaming down her face, her vest clinging damply to her, the Blonde went through her ritual, as aware as Erika and everyone else that she was jumping for survival, ran in too slowly, hit the bar with her shoulder, and was out.

Holding her head high, she collected her bag and walked off, getting a friendly pat on the shoulder from Bloxen who caught

## The High Jump Competition

Erika's eye, looked at her coldly, and sat by the gawky girl who, almost unnoticed, had become a major threat.

Erika flushed, The look from Bloxen had been a flagrant declaration of war, the row of empty seats was a no man's land, and the talk between Bloxen and the Gawk an obvious hatching of a plot between two allies against a common enemy.

'Very well,' Erika thought. 'Plot away but I'll jump until I die. If I burst my heart I'll beat you both. Yes.'

The judges altered the bar and Erika drank glucose and wiped her face. 'You are at least third,' she thought. 'Whatever happens you have made it into the last three.' And that was something. After her first two jumps she would have cheerfully settled for that. But now it was not enough. Now, after battling her way this far she wanted to go further. She wanted to win.

'*Achtung*!' The judges called for the eighth round at a height of 1.71. Three girls left and the seats by the High Jump were filling as the word spread that a really cracking competition was developing.

The Gawk prepared for her jump. She looked strong, there was no doubt about that, long and sinewy with hard, thin muscles which might have been specially made for endurance. She rocked, leaned back, ran in, seeming all elbows and awkwardness, and cleared, jumping off the landing bed with a triumphant punch in the air and walking back with her high-stepping action to a loud 'well done!' from Bloxen.

But, Erika pondered, for all the Gawk's obvious strength and assurance, her technique was not good. Her approach varied wildly, almost eccentrically, and she was taking off for her jump almost at random. But mere lunging strength alone could not keep her clearing the bar for ever, that was certain. It was a minor miracle that she had come so far and she would be found out. Erika had no doubt about that, but for the moment her eyes were on Bloxen whose technique seemed well nigh perfect and whose nerve appeared to be unbreakable.

Bloxen stood at her mark, icily cool, a marble statue brought

*Track and Field*

to life, and ran, and even Erika had to admit that it was not the best moment to go. Although the High Jump was tucked away from the runners' starting line, a sprint relay was taking place. The third leg of the race was at an angle to the bar but visible from the corner of one's eye, and as Bloxen went into her run the sprinters came hurtling down the track. To a terrific racket of shouts, batons were exchanged, a runner fell, the crowd roared, and Bloxen brought down the bar.

She walked back, her cold features for once almost showing emotion, and passed Erika who gave her a look as haughty as those she had herself received. Bloxen turned her head away but Erika did not mind that. 'Look away as much as you like,' she thought, 'but you failed, you . . . you iceberg!'

Erika poised herself and took a long, long look at the bar. 1.71 was a good height there was no doubt about that, after all it was as high as a fairly tall woman. But she had done it in the gym, and often, and she could do it now, and with Bloxen having failed at last now was the time to do it again. For the first time in the competition she was in a position to put the screw on Bloxen, and a good clearance, a really good one, would make Bloxen as edgy as she herself had been for the past ninety minutes, and then maybe that icy composure would crack, and then, maybe, that technique might not be as flawless as it appeared. And a really good jump would give the Gawk something to think about too.

With those thoughts in her mind, Erika went for the bar, *attacked* it as Fräulein Silber would have said, hit her marks perfectly, rose, turned, arched her back, cleared the bar with her head, her shoulders, her seat, her thighs and calves, and clipped it with her endlessly trailing heel and brought it down.

For a moment, for one devastating moment, as she lay on the landing bed, Erika was tempted to walk out of the arena. With all the odds in her favour she had failed to beat Bloxen on a jump and now, she felt it in her bones, she would walk out of the competition a third, and a poor third at that; and, as insidious as a virus, the thought came to her that she could pretend that she

# The High Jump Competition

was hurt. Nothing could be easier. She could limp back to her chair pretending that her old injury was back, retire with honour, and be greeted, not with disdain or ridicule, but with sympathy and understanding.

She came near to doing that. As she began what seemed to be a mile long trudge back to her chair she almost let her left leg buckle, but, from the spectators came a huge, hoarse bellow. 'You can do it, Erika!'

Erika peered into the darkness across the track. She could, or thought she could, vaguely make out her family. And as, dripping with sweat, Erika reached her chair, she remembered what her mother had said to her about honour.

Yes, that was a word to conjure with, honour, and Erika knew that if she cheated now she would never be able to look anyone in the face again, and so she walked firmly to her chair, wiped herself, sat down, and watched Bloxen take her second jump and clear, and, racing to the bar, cleared it also.

'And now,' she thought, as the bar went up again to 1.74, 'the battle is really on.'

And the Gawk failed, misjudging her run and trying to turn away at the last moment. But the judges declared that her whirling arm had crossed underneath the bar and so was a fault. And Bloxen failed, too, running immaculately but clipping the bar and bringing it down. But Erika, the bellow of encouragement ringing in her ears, cleared. So she could sit back and watch the others sweat it out.

She could also do a little thinking about the next rounds. One thing was certain: if it did come to a tie, if she, Bloxen and the Gawk failed three times at the same height, then she would be in a dull third place. She had lost count of her failures but she knew that she had more, and a lot more, than either of the other two girls. The only way she was going to win was to win outright, to out-jump both her opponents, and that, she was beginning to realize, was to be partly a psychological battle; if, now, she showed nervousness or loss of confidence, that would make the others feel stronger and more confident. No, the thing to do was

*Track and Field*

what Bloxen had done from the first round, stamp her authority on the competition and make the other two girls feel inferior, losers at these really challenging heights.

'So,' Erika said to herself. 'Now we'll try it the other way round.' And as the Gawk went for her second jump, Erika leaned back in her chair, her hands behind her head, affecting, though not feeling, mild boredom, as if now the result was preordained, with herself as the inevitable winner.

But it did not quite work out like that. In her clumsy way the Gawk cleared, and in her fluent way so did Bloxen, and the bar went up three more centimetres; and from the corner of her eye Erika saw that Herr Wolf and Fräulein Carow had come across the arena and were sitting a few metres away from the bar.

For a moment or two Erika did not take in the significance of that, assuming that as the High Jump had turned into a good tussle they were interested as any athlete would be in a good event. It was only when the board was held up with 1 metre 77 on it that she realized what was happening: they were now going into really good, first-class heights, and records were beckoning, and everyone was interested in those – particularly the masters of sport in the G.D.R. In 1983 the sixteen to seventeen-year-old girls' group at the Junior Spartakiad had been won by a jump of 1.79. That had been an exceptionally poor height, of course, the fifteen-year-old group had been won at 1.86. But still the bar called for a good leap.

The presence of Herr Wolf and Fräulein Carow was an added pressure but Erika tried to maintain her new pose of distinterest as the Gawk jumped the new height, and failed, and Bloxen went, and failed, and she went, and failed also.

But waiting for the Gawk to jump again, Erika was curiously undisturbed at her own failure. The bar was as much a psychological barrier as a physical one, and better jumpers than she could ever hope to be had failed at this height at her age only to go on triumphantly to world records. And besides, she felt that her jump had been good so that, despite her growing

## The High Jump Competition

fatigue, her technique was holding up under pressure. It remained to be seen whether the other girls would react in the same way.

But, disconcertingly, they did. The Gawk cleared the bar but only just, and Bloxen, although Erika did not miss the look of relief on that iceberg's face as she made her way back to her chair; but Erika hoped that it changed to a look of dismay as she too cleared.

Round eleven; heat, sweat, the sickly smell of talcum powder, and the bar going up to 1 metre 80 and Erika, knowing that she had cleared that height before in the gym, with Herr Wolf watching, waited her turn and wondered whether the Gawk and Bloxen had. Bloxen still looked dangerous and the Gawk seemed as if she could jump over the moon if she had a fit of inspiration; and she had one on her first jump, making a gigantic leap which brought a gasp from the crowd, and landing in a strange tangle of limbs. But she was clear, unlike Bloxen who failed and, unfortunately for herself, Erika, who took off too soon and caught the bar with her wrist. Bloxen cleared on her second jump, although it seemed to Erika a leap without inspiration, and Erika cleared, too.

The judges huddled around the bar, the giant ruler was brought out, the landing bed inspected, and, as Erika sat alone, Bloxen and the Gawk sat together, deep in conversation.

But her isolation did not bother Erika. Since the stocky girl had gone out she had not exchangd a word with anyone. But she was still in the competition and, she hoped, looking as though the next height, in the twelfth round, to be attempted after nearly two hours, was not one to terrify *her*; the trouble being that it did not look as if it was terrifying the others, either. But then, she thought, perhaps they were bluffing too, or – disturbing idea – perhaps *they* were not!

In any case she was about to find out as the Gawk took up her ungainly stance, ran, and in a blur of elbows and knees, failed, returning with a disconsolate air as if she knew that she was

*Track and Field*

facing an impossible task. Then Bloxen went forward, took her time, ran in her beautifully collected way, but brought the bar down just the same.

And Erika brought down the bar, too, but as she walked back she was warm inside as well as outside; despite the heat, tiredness, nervous strain, competition against real opposition, and hostility, she knew that her jump had been good. If anything, and she was aware that in view of the fact that she had failed it seemed odd, her jump had been *too* good in the sense that it had been, as it were, mechanically correct, but that was not a bad thing at all. It showed that her technique was still holding up under pressure. And she was level still with the other girls in this round – and she was sure that the Gawk was going out, which would leave her one of two jumpers left; a change from that round – a lifetime ago it seemed – when she had actually considered faking an injury.

But, she reminded herself severely, she was anticipating since the Gawk had not yet taken her second jump, and neither had the imposing Bloxen, and neither had she herself.

'Don't count your chickens before they are hatched,' she said, but the Gawk did fail again, really crashing into the bar, and Bloxen, missing her run-up, was adjudged to have fouled, the judge tapping her hand to show that as the girl had veered away her hand had crossed under the bar, and that, Erika knew, was a genuine sign of cracking nerve – and cracking technique.

Bloxen came back to her chair, shaking her head, and went into an earnest discussion with the Gawk as Erika's number was shown – and once again she went to her mark.

She stood stock-still, breathing deeply and evenly, trying to block out every distraction and concentrating on the black and white bar.

'You've done it,' she said to herself. 'You've done this height. Herr Wolf said so in the gym. So do it now!'

And she did, hitting her marks perfectly, sprinting in to the bar, taking off perfectly, and knowing even as her head soared above the bar that she would clear it.

## The High Jump Competition

Although she doubted if there was much space between her and the bar, that did not disturb her as she walked triumphantly back to her chair. She had done it. She was over, and at her best ever competitive height, and now the Gawk and Bloxen had to face the bar again – and it was a last chance for both of them – and, although she felt slightly ashamed of herself for doing so, she willed that both of them would fail.

And it *was* the last chance for the Gawk. Although Bloxen walked to the mark with her, and gave her an encouraging clap on the shoulder, and although it was clear that she was concentrating as she had never, perhaps, done before, her eyes half-closed, her hands clenched, biting her lip, and although she bounced forward as though she were wearing spring-heeled shoes, the height was too much for her and she was out, a not ignoble third.

Or, perhaps, equal second, since Bloxen had to jump again, but whatever hopes she might have had in that direction were dashed as Bloxen cleared leaving, at last, herself and Erika head-on.

Head-on but hardly face to face for, as the judges fussed with the bar, the two girls sat at opposite ends of the row of chairs, and although Erika stared defiantly at Bloxen, Bloxen merely turned her head away; that gesture, as Erika, to whom contempt did not come easily, felt, being more effective than her own childish stare.

She sipped her glucose, trying to relax, breathing deeply as she had been taught, wishing that she could change her vest, wishing that she could have a shower, wishing that the competition was over – with herself as winner, of course – and then it occurred to her that a rather long delay was taking place.

She looked up. The judges were in an earnest huddle. One of them left the group with the odd half-run officials always seem to effect and returned with a man in a red blazer and white slacks, obviously a very senior official, quite probably the Field Referee himself. The man bowed his head, listened, waved Herr Wolf forward, listened to him, and then nodded, obviously in

*Track and Field*

agreement; the group broke up, and a judge, trim in white, her face grave, walked towards the two girls.

Erika's heart sank. With absolute certainty, she knew that she was going to be disqualified for some obscure infringement of the rules, a copy of which the judge held in her hand, and each and every one of which she knew that she had breached.

A few feet from the competitors' chairs the woman paused, her eyebrows raised in surprise at the distance between Erika and Bloxen and being, as it were, at the apex of a triangle, the corners of which were the two girls, she was uncertain which of them to approach. However, being an official, she solved the problem in an official manner by beckoning them to her.

Erika nervously, Bloxen with her ingrained coolness, walked forward and stood before the judge who looked at them severely.

'I am sorry,' she said, and Erika's heart, already in her shoes, sank into the floor. The judge's brown eyes moved from Erika to Bloxen, and back again, 'I – we – are sorry for this delay. But you know what the next jump is?'

The next jump? Erika began counting on her fingers – the tenth, eleventh, twelfth? – but arithmetic was not needed because, maddeningly, Bloxen knew.

'The junior record,' she said.

'Yes. Good.' The judge nodded approval. 'The junior record. We are going to announce it on the public address system. It won't take more than a minute or so. Please don't let it disturb your rhythm. Just sit and relax. Thank you.'

Erika's heart returned from the locker-room and resumed its normal place as the judge looked curiously at the two girls, made as if to speak, then merely nodded. 'Good luck,' she said. 'To both of you.'

She walked away holding up her hand and a muted but penetrating gong boomed across the arena three times, followed by a soft, woman's voice.

'*Meine Damen und Herren* – Ladies and Gentlemen. The final of the 4 by 400 metres Relay Race will be delayed as in the Girl's Junior High Jump Championship, the competitors, Comrades

## The High Jump Competition

Karen Bloxen and Erika Nordern, will be attempting to equal the national junior record for this event. Thank you.'

Applause, not, perhaps, echoed by the relay runners, reverberated around the arena. Number six was held aloft, Karen Bloxen pulled off her track suit and walked to her mark. For a moment or two she stood perfectly motionless, one leg a little extended, as coldly beautiful and composed as a Greek statue, and then, the statue coming to life, she moved, rocking, heel and toe, forearms extended, then ran forward with her smooth, powerful, high-legged run, hit the ground with her left foot, rose – and hit the bar.

An eerie muted murmur filled the arena as she rolled off the landing bed, walked to her chair, and pulled on her track suit, expressionless, almost, one might have said, indifferent.

Then eight was held up, a muted voice behind her called, 'Good luck,' and Erika walked to her mark, almost symbolically, it occurred to her, opposite from Bloxen's, Bloxen being a left-footed jumper and approaching the bar the other way round.

Without the pounding of feet on the track, the shouts of other athletes, the shrilling whistles, bells ringing, the calling of the crowd, the arena was hushed and expectant, and collecting herself at her mark, Erika wished that it wasn't. After jumping in the cheerful racket of the competitions all afternoon the silence, the watching eyes, and above all the sense of being the complete centre of attention brought its own, new pressure, and Erika remembered what Fräulein Silber had said: 'It's all very well jumping in a gym – but in a stadium, with 50,000 people watching – that's what sorts out the champions from the rest.' And although there were not 50,000 people in the stadium, 5,000 at the most, Erika understood the force of the remark. But there they were, those watching thousands, and here, willy-nilly, was she, and there was nothing she could do about it other than walking off – and there, gleaming black and white, at an impossible, ludicrous height, was the bar.

Erika blew out her breath and drew it back, right down to the bottom of her rib-cage. 'Concentrate,' she said. 'Concentrate,

*Track and Field*

concentrate, concentrate,' and ran, bouncing off her right foot, driving upwards, the arena swivelling as she twisted backwards, the lights spinning dizzily, her back arching, legs high, and she was over – and clear.

Barely aware of the applause and cheers, she knelt on the landing bed and raised her hands. 'I've done it!' she said. 'Done it, done it, done it! Equalled the record!'

Equalled it! She jumped to the floor, shaking her head, and ran across the arena to her parents, they on their feet, shouting and clapping, but a white-suited arm barred her way.

'Fräulein!' A judge waved her back. 'You must wait. Wait.' She pointed. 'The other competitor has to jump.'

'Ah, of course. Excuse me.' Erika tried to collect herself. She walked, bounced, back to her chair, jubilation in her heart and jubilation on her face, and not deigning to hide it from Bloxen who, as she approached, was pulling off her track suit.

'Now,' Erika thought. 'Now, Bloxen, *You* sweat it out.'

The arena quietened as Bloxen went for her second jump, still poised, cool and calm, her run fluid and her jump fluent, but not fluent enough as, to a groan from the crowd, she failed again.

She came back to her seat but did not put on her track suit, rubbing her legs vigorously with a towel. She took a mouthful of glucose from her flask and then, without a glance at Erika, went for her third jump.

For all Erika's antagonism towards Bloxen, she felt a flicker of admiration for her poise as she took her mark, and Bloxen needed all the poise she possessed as, in a dead hush, she stood, a solitary figure, knowing, as Erika very well knew also, that three centimetres, the width of two fingers, and those alone, stood between her and defeat. Two finger-widths, but that was enough although, as Erika leaped to her feet, her arm raised in a victor's salute, Bloxen rolled off the landing bed, to the bouncing of the bar, as composed as she had been when the competition had begun.

'And now I have done it,' Erika said, 'I *have*,' speaking aloud

## The High Jump Competition

although applause drowned her words as, ignoring Bloxen, both arms high in salutation, she ran to the track and embraced Fräulein Silber.

'Erika!' Fräulein Silber hugged her. 'Well done. Oh well done. What a triumph!'

'Thank you.' Tears spilled down Erika's cheeks.

'Thank *you*,' Fräulein Silber said. 'Now, are you ready?'

'Ready?' Erika was only half paying attention as she peered over Fräulein Silber's shoulder, looking for her family. 'Ready for what?'

'Why,' Fräulein Silber held Erika at arm's length. 'For your next jump.'

'What?' Erika stared at Fräulein Silber incredulously. 'Another jump? But I've won!'

Fräulein Silber smiled. 'Of course you have. But now to *break* the record.'

'Aah!' Erika understood. The winner of a championship was always given the chance to go on and try to break the record. 'Should I try?'

'Of course you must.' Fräulein Silber was not amused. 'It is expected of you. But now sit down, relax. I'll be allowed to sit with you. I'll be with you in a minute.'

She strode towards the judges who were gathered in a conclave, scrupulously checking their mark-sheets and Erika went back to her seat. As she got there Bloxen stood up.

'Congratulations,' she said and offered her hand.

Erika took the hand, touched it, rather. 'Thank you,' she said in a frigid voice and half turned away but, manners overriding distaste, and feeling a little more was needed, especially from the winner to the loser, added, 'hard luck.'

'Are you going again?' Bloxen asked.

'Yes.'

'Well, the best of luck,' Bloxen said. 'Break the record. I hope you do.'

'Do you?' Erika was incredulous.

*Track and Field*

'Of course I do.' Bloxen frowned, the first sign of naked emotion she had shown all afternoon. 'What's the matter with you, anyway?'

'With me?' Erika's temper, bottled up for the past long hours, flared. 'You mean what's the matter with you.'

Bloxen's frown deepened, and she looked formidable, too. 'With me?'

'You. Yes.' Erika gave an emphatic nod. She glanced over her shoulder. The judges were still conferring, Fräulein Silber and Herr Wolf with them. 'Don't think that I don't know. You were going to make a fool of me. Oh, I heard about that – and what you said about my school. And this afternnon, never a word to me but advising the other girls. *And* – ' but she stopped abruptly. 'This is ridiculous,' she thought. 'I've just won the Championship, I'm about to jump for the G.D.R. record, and here I am wrangling like a spoiled child.' Not for the first time that afternoon, she was surprised at herself, but she was even more surprised at what Bloxen said.

'I don't know what you're talking about.' Bloxen was unmistakably sincere.

'But – ' Erika frowned in her turn. 'But I was told – '

'I don't care what you were told,' Bloxen said. 'All I've ever said about you is that you had courage coming back from an injury and I was looking forward to meeting you. And I did – want to meet you. But what happened? You turned your back on me. You didn't even answer when I said "good luck".'

'You shouted that? Oh dear.' Erika sat down with a bump. 'I thought that it was Fräulein Carow.' She looked up, crimson with embarrassment. 'I don't know what to say. I mean . . . I do really. I'm sorry. Really and truly sorry. But I was told. . . . '

Bloxen smiled, the smile transforming her cold features. 'You were psyched.'

'Psyched?'

'Yes. Your coach gave you an enemy. Someone to go against. And it worked.'

Erika shook her head. 'But that isn't fair.'

## The High Jump Competition

'Never mind. It didn't affect me, did it? You won because you were better on the day. Now go and break the record. We'll meet again, as friends.'

The conclave of judges was breaking up and Fräulein Silber and Herr Wolf were coming towards the girls. Bloxen gave Erika a clap on the shoulder. 'Do it. And my name is Karen.'

The gong boomed mellifluously as Fräulein Silber and Herr Wolf stood over Erika.

*'Meine Damen und Herren. . . .'*

'Well done, Erika,' Herr Wolf said. 'And the best of luck.'

Fräulein Silber vigorously massaged Erika's legs as the public address system announced that Comrade Nordern was going to attempt to beat the Junior Indoor Record.

'Now, Erika,' Fräulein Silber turned her muscular attention to Erika's arms. 'I'll be with you for this round. You have three attempts so don't worry if you fail the first time. *Drive* as you jump. *Drive!*'

Silence as Erika walked to her mark, another race delayed and the entire arena, from the Deputy Mayor himself down to the children acting as helpers, hushed and watching; the Nordern family not in their seats but on the edge of them.

And, the centre of attention, standing at her mark and feeling as lonely as Robinson Crusoe, stood Erika, in that place where all the good will and good wishes in the world could not help her, looking at the distant bar over which only her own skill and courage and strength could take her.

And on her first jump they were not enough. The bar came down at the merest brush of Erika's heel, and they were not enough on the second jump, either, as she made a bad turn and caught the bar with her hip.

Erika sat with Fräulein Silber as the bar was replaced, drained and spent, not so much physically, although she was that, as mentally, feeling that one more sight of the bar would make her be sick.

'I can't do it,' she said.

'You *can*.' Fräulein Silber poured glucose down Erika's throat

*Track and Field*

and kneaded her legs and arms. 'You can do it. One centimetre. Just one, and you have the record. One more jump. Just one. It's in your mind, Erika. *Will* yourself to clear.'

'I'll try,' Erika said, as her number was held up. 'I really will try.'

She walked to the mark with leaden legs and leaden arms, for all the glucose her mouth dry although the rest of her was sopping wet, and looked at the bar and thought of the mocking, tantalizing centimetre which stood between her and the record book.

'I *can* do it,' she whispered as she launched herself forward, running, as she felt, in slow motion, the bar appearing to come to her rather than she to it, willing herself to clear it, pulling out every one of her last ebbing resources, snatching a last breath as she took off, head, shoulders, hips, rising above the bar, thighs, calves clearing as she fell backwards, but, to a huge, collective groan, her heel catching the bar and, as she fell, it falling with her.

Erika lay on her back, staring at the lights and the rafters to sympathetic applause, and for the first time in her life she swore. '*Verdammt!*' she said. 'Damn it! Damn it! Lost by a millimetre. *Verdammt!*'

But she was given little time to repine. As whistles blew and starting-pistols cracked, and the cheerful row of the competitions restarted. Fräulein Silber hustled her out of the arena and down into the locker-room.

'Celebrations afterwards,' she said, 'when you get your medal. Have a hot shower and change. Quickly, before you get cold and stiffen up.'

The locker door proved to be as hard to open as it had been to close, but eventually, glowing from the shower and in clean clothes, Erika sat on the bench again.

'Here,' Fräulein Silber handed over a flask of hot, milky, very sweet coffee, and a bar of chocolate. 'Get these down you. No need to watch your diet for a while.'

# The High Jump Competition

Erika obediently drank and ate, Fräulein Silber watching her intently.

'How do you feel?' she asked.

'Drained,' Erika said.

'That's natural.' Fräulein Silber pressed more chocolate on Erika. 'A long tough competition. It always seems an anticlimax afterwards – even when you've won.'

'I suppose so.' Sullenness was foreign to Erika's nature, but she sounded sullen as she spoke.

A little wrinkle appeared between Fräulein Silber's eyebrows. 'What's the matter? You're not fretting about the record, are you? Don't worry about that. To equal it was a tremendous achievement. Really tremendous.'

Erika looked down the shabby locker-room with its battered lockers and grimy pipes. 'It isn't that,' she said.

'No? Then what is it?'

Erika took a deep breath. 'It's about Bloxen. Frau Milch should not have said what she did. Karen didn't say anything about me, or the school.'

'Oh.' Fräulein Silber looked grave. 'She told you then?'

'Yes.'

'And?'

Erika raised her head. 'I don't think it was right. It was cheating.'

'Cheating!' Fräulein Silber looked decidedly cross.

'Yes.' Erika stared defiantly at Fräulein Silber. 'We're supposed to regard our opponents with respect, aren't we? Respect and in a spirit of comradely fairness. That's what the books say, isn't it? But it wasn't fair or comradely to send me out despising a nice girl. Was it?'

Fräulen Silber looked away, a trace of sadness on her face. 'No, perhaps it wasn't.'

'Perhaps.' Erika was little short of contemptuous.

'There's really no need for that tone of voice,' Fräulein Silber was sharp. She glanced at her watch and obviously decided they

## Track and Field

had a little time to spare. 'Erika, I'm sorry, but I was worried about you. I knew that you had everything, courage, stamina, technique, but I didn't think that you had . . . had the killer instinct. So I thought . . . well. . . . '

'Well?' Erika deliberately turned the phrase round. 'It wasn't well. Not well at all. And as for that other thing – the *killer* instinct – I don't want to have it.'

'It worked though,' Fräulein Silber said. 'You won.'

'I might have won anyway,' Erika said. 'I don't want to win by tricks. I want to do it on my own merits.'

'But you did win,' Fräulein Silber pressed her point.

'Winning isn't everything,' Erika said. 'And if I had been friendly to Karen she might have helped me. She was helping the others. I might have broken the record then.'

'Yes, you might have done,' Fräulein Silber admitted ruefully. 'But you have to be hardened, you know. When, and I mean when, when you go into international competitions, when you meet athletes from the capitalist world, then you'll have to go through the fire.'

'I don't want to hear about the capitalist world.' Erika gestured impatiently. 'For all I know they're as nice as Karen. I'd sooner loose in a socialist way than win like that.'

Fräulein Silber sighed. 'All right. All right. But promise me one thing.'

An hour ago Erika would have promised unhesitatingly and without qualification but now she said, 'What?'

Fräulein Silber noticed that, and clearly didn't like it. But still she spoke in a quiet, reasonable tone. 'Don't say this to anyone else until you've thought about it and spoken to me again.'

Erika thought for a moment. It wasn't an unreasonable request and she did want to think the matter over, and, clinching her argument, Fräulein Silber said, 'You don't want to spoil your family's day, do you?'

No, Erika certainly didn't want to do that and so, as the public address called the winners of the Girls' High Jump to the rostrum, she agreed.

## The High Jump Competition

'Thank you.' Fräulein Silber stood up. 'Time to go, but I'll tell you one thing Erika. You'll feel differently when you go on to the rostrum.'

As Erika entered the arena to applause and walked to the victors' rostrum, followed by Karen and the Gawk, she did feel rather different. The halo of stardom was on her head and it felt comfortable and when, on the rostrum, she dipped her head and the Deputy Mayor slipped a medal around her neck and kissed her cheek, and when Karen and the Gawk warmly shook hands and said, 'Well done, you won fair and square,' she was beginning to feel that Fräulein Silber had not been far wrong, after all; and when, freed from officialdom, but still glowing from the congratulations of Herr Wolf and Fräulein Carow, she went to her rapturous family, she was beginning to think that she had been too hasty by half in judging her coach.

Rapturous her family was, too. Her mother embraced her in a bear-like hug and her father, standing back in his shy way, had moist eyes behind his thick spectacles. Surrounded by admirers, Erika was ushered out – and by the time she had been handed into the car, what remained of her scruples had quite gone; for the time being, at any rate.

*Track and Field*

# A Girl Called Golden

*David Bateson*

When only 18, Betty Cuthbert won gold medals for the 100 metres, 200 metres and 100-metres relay in the 1956 Melbourne Olympics, then the gruelling 400-metre race eight years later in Tokyo. The breaker of 16 world records, she was given the nickname 'Golden Girl' and was decorated by the Queen. Later the illness of multiple sclerosis afflicted her, and nowadays she lives a more secluded life in Western Australia.

Why did you run
   when your schoolmates were walking?
Why did you sprint
   if they started to run?
Why did you train
   while others were playing?
What was the secret
   that made it seem fun?

Was it the feel
   of the fresh air and sunshine?
Was it the stir
   of the breeze in your hair?
What made the coach
   recognize you were special?
Was it because
   you had courage to spare?

Showing your will
   when the muscles were aching,
Long spells of effort
   and much to be learned,
Heeding the words

  that some others rejected,
Knowing that winning
  could only be earned.

Time slipped away
  then came the Olympics;
Still in your teens
  but spurred on by the cheers;
Glory at last –
  as you gained your gold medals,
A time to remember
  the rest of your years.

*Track and Field*

# The Eighth Paralympic Games, Seoul 1988

*Bill Boyle*

The Eighth Paralympics followed the Olympic Games to Seoul, like a breath of fresh sporting air blowing away the squalid memories of the drug disqualifications and squabbles over professionalism. This was participation in its purest sense, in the truest sporting sense. Born without knees and lower legs, Karen Davidson is now 25 years old. She has just successfully represented Britain in the Seoul Paralympics. Her successes certainly didn't show on any medals tables, and didn't bring any banner headlines on the tabloid Sports Pages, but were successes for all that.

Karen competed in the 100, 200, 400, 800, 1500 and 3000 metres wheelchair races. In cold statistical terms her best results were three fourth places. Disappointing you might think for a girl who in the New York Games for the Disabled (1984) had won a Gold, a Silver and four Bronze medals.

'I'm disappointed in a way, but my mother keeps reminding me that I was the fourth best in the world,' is Karen's typical response. Further emphasis of her versatility is provided by the fact that her New York medals were for field events (shot, discus and javelin) and in the swimming pool.

'I'd never sat in a wheelchair until I went to New York, but the racing looked such good fun I thought I'd give it a go.' Such good fun! Did such thoughts even cross the minds of the participants in the Modern Olympics, or has the pressure to succeed at all costs, removed the sense of fun and sport completely?

To further astonishment, Davidson completed her first

## The Eighth Paralympic Games, Seoul 1988

London Marathon in under four hours – a mere four days after getting her first wheelchair! 'I've since competed in a dozen marathons,' said Davidson, who holds the women's wheelchair record for the London event. 'The atmosphere and sense of achievement are something special.' You can say that again!

Karen's enduring memories of the Paralympics in Seoul? 'The opening and closing ceremonies are fantastic. I can't explain what it was like to walk into the stadium in front of that crowd of a hundred thousand people as part of the British team. Most of us were in tears. It was an occasion we'll remember for the rest of our lives.'

The contrast is all too evident with the opening ceremonies of recent Modern Olympics, which many of the competitors, deriding the loss of training time, have failed to attend at all.

Sport is definitely going wrong somewhere. Some priorities need re-evaluating against the principles shown by the likes of Karen Davidson and her fellow Paralympians.

Sting in the tail. Karen had to give up her full-time job in order to compete in the Paralympics. Perhaps the sponsors who fatten the bank balances of our pampered 'stars' need to look into their consciences too!

# *But Is It Sport?*

# Pop's Boy

*Irvin Ashkenazy*

In the small hours of a dark September morning I dropped off the truck that had brought me as far as the north Florida town of Lake City. Going into an all-night lunch-room, I let my suitcase drop and ordered a hamburger.

The only other customer was an elderly man eating a bowl of soup. He looked at me a moment. He smiled as he saw the University of Florida labels on my suitcase.

'Don't I see you at the U in St Augustine one night last spring?' he asked. 'You win the state amateur heavyweight title.'

I nodded.

The old man stopped. He then added, 'You don't have them scars over your eyes then.' I'd turned pro, I told him.

'You quit school?'

'No, I turned pro to stay in school.'

After a while the old man swung off his stool. 'If you're going to the University,' he suggested, 'I can take you. I'm going through Gainesville.'

As his jalopy rattled down Highway 41, Pop strung stories about the great fighters of the past. He'd trained and managed fighters since 1910. He was now retired 'in a way'. But he was helping a promoter by looking for a heavyweight to fight Kayo Billy Terry in a ten-round main bout at Tampa the next evening. Terry's scheduled opponent had broken his hand training the day before.

By now the darkness was becoming dawn. I told Pop that I wasn't actually stopping at Gainesville. I would hitch a ride from there to Miami. 'I thought you was going back to school,' he said.

I was. But first I had to collect some money from a man named Willie. He was payoff man for a manager who had taken me with his stable of fighters on a barnstorming tour. At the close of the tour he had disappeared. I had about 500 dollars coming to me. Miami was Willie's home territory. If he wasn't there, I'd wait for him, picking up fights to keep myself going.

'Forget it,' Pop said gruffly. 'Charge it off to education.'

If I didn't get that money, I said, I wouldn't get any education. I needed 300 dollars to pay off my debts from the previous year so I could get started this year.

Another silence. Then, 'Who'd you fight this summer?'

I mumbled a few names.

'You didn't fight them? Them's all tough, main-go boys!'

I explained how the barnstorming manager had matched me in ten-round main bouts from the start.

'The louse!' Pop muttered. 'Throwing in a green amateur with guys like those! You stay the limit with any of them monkeys?'

I drew a dog-eared sheaf of newspaper clippings from my wallet. Pop nearly wrecked the car trying to drive and read at the same time. 'I'll be darned,' he muttered to the windshield. 'You win them all!' After a few moments he turned to me. 'Stay over in Tampa and I'll put you in against Terry tonight! You'll get your 300 dollars.'

Pop's landlady looked at Pop. 'Is he the one to fight Billy?' she asked.

'He's my boy,' Pop said brusquely. She gave me something to eat. Then I went to Pop's room and hit the hay.

When I woke up, the bedroom windows were filled with night. A stocky, baggy-eyed little man was bent over me, his fingers plucking at the muscles in my legs. 'This is J.D., my trainer,' Pop explained. J.D., it turned out, also drove a cab.

While I was dressing I told Pop that the last I'd heard of Terry was a couple of years before. He'd been pretty good. I wondered what he'd done since.

'He's disgraced the name he's fighting under,' Pop said bitterly. 'Tonight he's trying to make a comeback. All that means is he's going to try to win because nobody's paying him to lay down!' When I asked if he could still fight if he wanted to, Pop nodded slowly. 'He might have been heavyweight champ, if he'd listened to me – ' I must have shown my surprise. 'I used to manage him,' Pop said gruffly.

A mounting roar swept through the walls of the dressing room. 'The semifinal's over,' J.D. commented. Pop threw an arm across my shoulders and said, 'This boy you're fighting is good. He can hit and he can box. But he does his training in dance halls. Hold him for six rounds and he's through! But until then – watch it! He's tricky and he's dirty.'

As I moved out at the clang of the bell, Terry charged across the ring. I stepped back, half-crouching, and caught everything on arms, gloves and shoulder. I let him come, moving in a circle. When he closed in I tangled his arms without clinching.

After the initial flurry, Terry knew that I was no amateur. He was desperate now. He needed to win so badly.

Suddenly he put his thumb into my eye. I hunched against the ropes, unable to see. Terry's brain-rattling blows jolted against the back of my head and smashed down on my kidneys. I managed to fall into a clinch. Terry pulled out with a vicious butt of his head to my brow. Then the bell clanged.

Pop protested the foul to the referee. But the referee only shrugged. Apparently he hadn't seen it.

During the second round, Terry rushed me. I backed up. But he closed in, seizing my arms at the elbows. Locked face to face, he said, 'Fight! You yellow punk!' and he spat full in my face.

I could only look at him. I flung him from me; clean across the ring he went, into the ropes and bounded off them as I came charging in.

Next thing I knew, I lay upon a cloud, floating in space.

# Pop's Boy

I heard a distant voice say, 'Six!' 'Seven!' At 'Eight!' I got to one knee, and at 'Nine! I was on my feet.

Terry moved in fast now, trying for the finishing blow. I smothered his attack, turning so that his back was finally on the ropes. Letting my full 220 pounds sag against him, I dragged him along the strands, knowing they were burning welts across his back. In close, I stamped on his feet. The punches I was pumping into Terry had little shock power. But I was striking with the heel of the hand instead of the knuckles. The glove laces left raw places with every blow. When the referee managed to crash between us, I struck on the break. He staggered. I followed through in a hook that cracked against Terry's jaw. He plunged to the floor.

I climbed through the ropes, hardly waiting to hear the end of the count. Pop moved suddenly into the ring, lifted Terry in his arms and dragged him into his corner.

Pop and I went to a little restaurant afterward. He looked very tired as he gave me a roll of bills. I counted 300 dollars, then peeled off 75 dollars and handed it to him. 'What's that for?' he asked. I told him it was 25 per cent, the regular agent's cut. He pushed the money toward me. 'You don't owe me nothing, son.'

Presently I said: 'I'm sorry I had to fight dirty. You saw what he did.' Pop nodded. He wasn't looking at me.

'You figure on graduating?'

I told him I guessed so, surprised at the question.

'You graduate. Make something of yourself.'

J.D. hurried up and said to Pop, 'We'll just about make the Gainesville bus. Ain't you coming to the station with us?' Pop just sat there. 'Tell you the truth,' he sighed, 'I'm kind of beat up.' I grasped his hand. 'So long, Pop – and thanks a million.'

At the bus station J.D. shook my hand. 'Pop'll get busy and line up another bundle of easy cabbage for you pretty soon.' I told him that tonight's "cabbage" wasn't easy. But it was certainly the fastest three hundred I'd ever made. J.D.'s baggy eyes for a moment were baffled.

*But Is It Sport?*

Then the sad smile glimmered. 'You don't have to put on no dog with me, boy. I seen the promoter give Pop the 130 bucks for your 20 per cent of the gate.'

Before I could speak, the bus burst into a roar. J.D. shoved me aboard.

Next day I wrote Pop asking him about the 170 dollars he must have taken out of his own pocket. I couldn't remember the address of his boarding-house, so I sent it in care of the arena. I wrote him twice more, but all my letters were returned marked, 'Not here.'

Two months later I received a wire from J.D. offering me a Tampa main-go. He met me at the bus station and hurried me into his cab. 'How's Pop?' I asked.

J.D. paused in mid-motion. 'Didn't you know? Pop's dead.'

I felt as though someone had kicked me in the stomach.

I asked him when it happened and he said, 'The next morning, after you went back to Gainesville. His landlady found him in bed, dead.' He tapped his chest. 'Just gave out, I reckon.'

It was a moment or two before I could speak again. 'Did Pop have any family?'

'Just that one kid,' J.D. said.

'What kid?'

J.D. looked at me sharply. And a funny look came over his face.

'Didn't you know? Billy Terry was Pop's son.'

# Who Killed Davey Moore?

*Bob Dylan*

Who killed Davey Moore?
Why an' what's the reason for?

'Not I,' says the referee,
'Don't point your finger at me.
I could have stopped it in the eighth
And maybe kept him from his fate,
But the crowd would've booed, I'm sure,
At not getting their money's worth.
It's too bad he had to go,
But there was pressure on me too, you know.
It wasn't me that made him fall,
No, you can't blame me at all.'

'Not us,' says the angry crowd,
Whose screams filled the arena loud.
'It's too bad he died that night
But we just like to see a fight.
We didn't mean for him to meet his death.
We just meant to see some sweat.
There ain't nothing wrong in that.
It wasn't us that made him fall,
No, you can't blame us at all.'

'Not me,' says his manager,
Puffing on a big cigar,
'It's hard to say, it's hard to tell,
I always thought that he was well.

## But Is It Sport?

It's too bad for his wife an' kids he's dead,
But if he was sick, he should've said.
It wasn't me that made him fall,
No, you can't blame me at all.'

'Not me,' says the gambling man,
With his ticket stub still in his hand,
'It wasn't me that knocked him down –
My hands never touched him none.
I didn't commit no ugly sin;
Anyway I put money on him to win.
It wasn't me that made him fall,
No, you can't blame me at all.'

'Not me,' says the boxing writer,
Pounding print on his old typewriter,
Sayin' 'Boxing ain't to blame –
There's just as much danger in a football
  game.'
Sayin' 'Fist fighting is here to stay,
It's just the old American way.
It wasn't me that made him fall,
No, you can't blame me at all.'

'Not me,' says the man whose fists
Laid him low in a cloud of mist,
Who came here from Cuba's door
Where boxing ain't allowed no more.
'I hit him, yes, it's true,
But that's what I am paid to do.
Don't say "murder", don't say "kill",
It was destiny, it was God's will.'

# Glove me Tender

*Kolton Lee*

As a public spectator sport, women's boxing is almost unheard of and, among those who have heard of it, it is viewed with at best curiosity, but at worst thinly concealed disgust. Most traditionally male-sports have accepted women's changing role in society and their various governing bodies have openly encouraged women's participation. Boxing is different. Women's boxing is not even recognized by the British Boxing Board of Control (BBBC) or the Amateur Boxing Association (ABA). John Morris, General Secretary of the BBBC, admits that as a body they do not even have a stance on women's boxing. Officially it doesn't exist. 'Personally, I'm not in favour,' he says. 'I don't think it's a sport for the ladies. Certainly I wouldn't want my wife or daughter to do it.'

Joe Lewis, Secretary of the ABA, agrees with him. 'We don't approve of women boxing. Physiologically and psychologically, women are not made for boxing.'

A comment made from the trainer at the Thomas A Becket gym is something of a contradiction in terms. 'Personally, I don't agree with women's boxing. I think it's crazy. I don't really enjoy working with women. My attitude to women is that they really belong at 'ome. But I agree with women's boxing as long as they're dedicated and want to do it.'

Twenty-six-year-old Sue Atkins is nothing if not dedicated. She has been boxing now for some seven years. 'What makes Sue so good is that she is so aggressive,' he says. 'She's a strong, very powerful woman.'

Fine features, contrasting sharply with strong arms and well-defined leg muscles, Sue is Britain's unofficial featherweight champion. Unofficial, because without even a comprehensive list of female boxers in the country, the title is somewhat spurious. But who cares? She's had nine fights, won seven and lost two.

Sue began boxing after trying her hand at a self-defence and kick-boxing club. But she soon developed a taste for straight boxing. The fact that men box and women don't didn't really come into it.

'I used to do netball and all that stuff but I got hurt more then, with split eyes and elbows in the face, than I've ever got boxing. Women's boxing is artistic in a way. A woman's body flows better than a man's.'

Sue feels her dedication is

*But Is It Sport?*

---

constantly undermined by the boxing authorities. 'If you're not careful you can get a lot of undercover dealings in the game which is why I wish the sport could move out into the open. All the time it is pushed underground people get pushed around; fighters aren't treated fairly by promoters.'

Karen Hope is another woman throwing jabs at the boxing establishment. Initially attracted to a sport that was 'a bit different,' she enjoys it mainly for the training. 'You get real exhilaration from battering a boxing bag.'

'I have doubts about boxing as a sport – two people whacking the hell out of each other – but then I don't want to fight. I just enjoy the training.'

# A-Hunting I Will Go, Without Shame

K. M. Peyton

I live deep in the country where the horse, hunting, and the pony club has a strong hold. I work hard, and keeping a horse is my one dear indulgence. It has taken me nearly fifty years to get to own my dream-horse, nearly too long to acclimatize to the riding of it – not quite but breaking my back in a fall nine months ago and coming back again after the lay-off has emphasized afresh how much riding means to me, what spiritual resources are to be drawn from riding off the roads, through the bridleways, over the stubble. Walking does it too, but being on a horse adds an extra dimension, and cements through long hours of each other's company the relationship between horse and rider which brings such satisfaction.

However, I do sometimes go hunting too. I adore hunting and am not ashamed to admit it. One Saturday a few weeks ago I sat on my mare in a small wood on the top of a hill overlooking a river estuary. It was a morning of very high tide, of bright sunshine, but bitterly cold. Ahead the green grass stretched to meet the sky and on either side, both inland and to seaward, it sloped away down to the seawalls and sheets of waveflecked water which seemed to fill the landscape as far as the eye could see. Good enough just to sit there drinking it in – from a viewpoint one normally has no access to – but then to see hounds stream down over the grass followed breakneck by the bright coats of the huntsman and whippers-in, feel the mare's excitement, wanting to go but having to hold her back until it was the field's turn, cantering slowly at first and then being overtaken and, striding out faster and faster down the hill in a great melee of horses like the Charge of the Light Brigade, knowing there was a hedge at the bottom and one had to stay in control somehow . . . after five days of desk work to feel the adrenalin running like that is indescribable . . . see the bars in the hedge loom and feel the mare's wild effort, see your friend alongside and find yourself laughing because it is so marvellous . . . how can you not love it, if you do it?

But of course if you don't do it you only see the hunting people when they are on the roads and holding up the traffic (a very small part of the day), enjoying them-

127

## But Is It Sport?

selves when other people are working.

If hunting people did not so obviously enjoy hunting, but did it as a duty, would they attract such a bad press?

I am always deeply suspicious that the cruelty-to-foxes angle of those against hunting is only part of the argument. I think they partly resent fox-hunters enjoying the sport so much and looking as if they are superior and rich and privileged. Anyone on a horse is forced to look down on anyone not on a horse, so is willy-nilly superior. Quite a lot of hunting people are rich – all sports have their rich and poor – but contrary to common opinion not all fields are made up entirely of Prince Charles and his friends. The hunt I belong to is small and unfashionable and most of the followers are farmers who hunt to have a day off with their friends at the season of the year when they can afford the time. Hunting takes place from November to March in the worst of the weather when the mud is deep, the rain cold. Sunny days are a bonus.

Yes, it is cruel to kill a fox with a pack of hounds, but is it more cruel than to kill with a gun or strangle it in a snare? Hounds kill a fox quickly if they catch it, but guns and snares often do terrible damage without killing. Foxes breed too readily to go unculled. A farmer in our village has shot over twenty this winter.

In our local paper last week there was a letter exhorting protesters to demonstrate at the Boxing Day meet. In the same paper is an advertisement offering good prices for winter fox pelts. A wood near my home is full of fox snares to try to satisfy this same advertiser. (My daughter, home for the weekend, walking the dog, was told to keep the dog out of the wood in case it got in a snare.) Do the foxes caught in these snares lie down and die peacefully? Nobody is holding demonstrations concerning their much more lingering and agonizing deaths. Why not?

Presumably because nobody is having a good time in the killing, merely making money, which is a much more understandable motive and therefore not worth making a fuss about.

# Moral Rules to Every Game

*Sam Ramsamy*

Sportsmen and women have been asked to exercise their conscience in the face of South Africa's political system of apartheid, which blights the lives of black people, and arguably those of white people, too. That system is as solidly in place as ever and applies repression with even greater force than in the past. The government systematically denies black people their political rights and all evidence of dissent is suppressed.

This is the first reason for not playing sport against South Africa. It underlies the appeal by Commonwealth governments, the United Nations and others in favour of a general boycott until South Africa's government respects basic political and human norms. It is not an argument confined to sport or South Africa. Only last week the British government persuaded Everton FC not to tour in China.

It is sometimes said that sport is 'special' and political norms should not apply. This suggests that athletes are different from doctors, soldiers, teachers or parents; that athletes are less thinking, less fully human, than other people, I do not accept this condescending assumption.

Recent international law has reinforced the view that professional people cannot escape moral responsibility by appealing to their professional status. This is surely equally true of athletes.

The Canadian sprinter, Ben Johnson, may have been put under pressure to take drugs by other competitors, or led on by his coach and doctor; but he took the decision and is responsible in law, as an athlete and a person.

If doctors have the Hippocratic Oath and soldiers the Geneva Convention, sport also recognizes a code of moral conduct, symbolized by the Olympic ideal and summarized as 'fair play'.

The appeal to rules, to justice and equality is fundamental to sport and explains why South Africa has been and remains its most controversial area. This is why the campaign to isolate its sport has been so successful, and those who claim the boycott campaign unfairly pillories South Africa miss this point. It is why the Olympic Movement and most sports organizations have suspended or banned South Africa from their competitions.

It is wrong to say that sport is

morally or politically neutral. It is, in fact, passionate about certain values of equality and non-discrimination. It is fair to challenge players, including those who want to tour South Africa, and to criticize their actions if they fall short of sport's own moral standards.

It is sometimes argued that campaigns to stop tours deny the players' individual liberties. Colin Moynihan, the British Minister for Sport, recently went out of his way to say that the Government would not withdraw the rebel cricket tour members' passports, condemning the demand as anti-libertarian.

The non-racial sports movement says the appeal of one right must be set against other rights: such as those of all South Africans to enjoy *their* freedoms. Those who promote British cricketers' right to freedom of movement or employment should be reminded that in South Africa black sportsmen frequently cannot travel because their passports are impounded. They certainly do not earn a living from sport on the same terms as white players. Whose rights matter most? Whose needs are greater?

The non-racial sports movement is struggling to defend the most basic social and economic rights. British cricketers will not suffer extreme poverty if they do not play in South Africa. What they are defending is cream on the cake, the luxury that visiting tourists are guaranteed by their grateful hosts.

In the last resort, the issue of South Africa is irredeemably political. Sportsmen and women cannot escape that fact, any more than international sports associations and governments. Like it or not, foreign sports tours will be exploited by the South African government and profoundly resented by most South Africans. Yes, cricketers in Britain and rugby players belonging to the International Rugby Board may go to South Africa: but the choice is a moral and political one. It invites condemnation on the grounds that South Africa violates the norms of acceptable political and sporting conduct; and involves taking the side of injustice and oppression.

# The Progress of Sport

*Raymond Wilson*

That the sport has dropped out of sport is alltoo certain.
God knows, mine was no Public School, splendidly living up
To some Latin motto, where the School (and Rugby) Captain
Roused his defeated side to three loud cheers,
And was cheered back by those who walked off with the Cup.
Far otherwise! Yet, on cindered spare ground where a black
   pit-heap rears,
We played a clean, hard game, and didn't grudge
The frothy pints we bought the 'opposition', after they'd
   'murdered' us.
We took our victories with nonchalance; our losses without fuss.

Earlier, in hooligan school playgrounds, where we'd tumbled
   and fought
Our way through childhood, we all of us learned the hard way
What bullying was, and set against it notions of 'fair play':
It got hammered into us, somehow, that to 'be a sport'
Had obscurely to do with personal honour,
With not abusing the whip hand when you'd got it,
With a regard for rules, truth, behaving decently.
(Seen this way, sport trains soul as well as body.)

And so, when Olympic Organizers, backed by Ministers
Of Sport, proclaimed it the means to International
Goodwill, a Cause common to All Humanity,
Clearing the way to Tolerance and Peace,
We shared their vaulting rhetoric, quite certain of success.

You know what followed: bickering declining by degrees
To ill-will, malice, slanderous accusation –

## But Is It Sport?

To extravagant rewards, immoderate blame –
To unconceded victories, discredited referees
(Try telling a gold medallist his whole world's just a game!) –
To violence, drug abuse and tortuous disputation.

Great States have stalked off the field, carrying like holy grails,
As any spoiled brat might do, ball, stumps and bails.

If Mankind's now lined up for the last high jump (World
 War Three),
You can bet your bottom dollar the conflagration
Will be sparked off by Sport, whose one clear object seems to be
To sharpen rivalries; set Nation against Nation.

## *Sport on TV*
## Points of View

On *Points of View* we get more letters on the subject of sport than on any other. Sportsmen and women, by the very nature of their enthusiasm, seem to be more active correspondents than people who write on other subjects, although it's fair to say the *anti-*sport lobby are just as vociferous. Mr D. R. Wardle of Southsea, writing on behalf of himself and a Miss Gail Sinclair, says –

> *Gail and I have got so tired of having sport* rammed *down our throats on all three channels – frequently at the same time – that we decided to find out what percentage of viewing time is taken up on this subject. Did you know that on a good week – I mean with less coverage than usual – that 43% of afternoon viewing and 27% of evening viewing over a seven day period was taken up with sport?*

Fair play it is then, as I hope to demonstrate by quoting this letter from Glen Griffiths of Norwich.

> *Generally a placid person I find myself forced to put a pen to paper in defence of the silly allegation that too many hours of television are devoted to sport.*
>
> *Having carefully taken into account the total number of television hours per week, I estimate that only 10% is actually given to sport! Surely no one can seriously consider this percentage so outrageous?*
>
> *I would suggest that those against sport, either switch off, turn over, or better still 'participate'. But I don't doubt that hearing the very word, 'participate' 100,000 viewers would probably collapse! Healthy body, healthy mind. Think about it! Please.*

*Sports on TV*

Here's Mrs D. S. Allnutt of High Wycombe, Bucks, still on the subject of sport on all channels.

> *Whilst I understand that you cannot be held responsible for Independent Television viewing, it seems to me that we should be able to expect a rather wider choice than that offered by BBC 1 and BBC 2. I understood that the second BBC channel was meant to enhance and widen the scope of viewing available to your audience. I can only assume that you have interpreted this to mean that you can now double the amount of sports coverage so that you can, therefore, attract the boxing enthusiast as well as the golfer.*
>
> *Of course, I may be wrong, but I am sure that I am not the only person amongst your audience who thinks that a choice between Sport, Sport, or Sport is no choice at all.*

And on the subject of commentators . . .

> *Why-oh-why do commentators have to open their big mouths?*
>
> *I refer of course to the ladies doubles badminton (*Grandstand – Saturday*). As soon as the British pair took the lead by only one point, Mister Barry Davies had to comment 'dare I say it, but the British girls now have the wind in their sails to win this game.'*
>
> *And what happens? The usual story – we lose the next three points and of course the game!!*
>
> *Please tell Mr Davies from me, 'no, you dare not say it, just shut up.'*

Dennis R. Hyde of Liskeard, Cornwall, writes on the subject of top crown bowls.

> *May I say how much I enjoy the BBC's Top Crown series, especially as it is so easily followed* with the volume turned down*! Harry Rigby's inane and childish remarks and phrases completely spoil the programme!*

## Points of View

Beatrice Saunders of Weybridge, Surrey, writes on the subject of tennis commentators.

*I dislike criticizing either the radio or television because there are so many excellent programmes but do you think someone would ask the tennis commentators to talk a little less. We cannot concentrate on the strokes or the tactics when we are given a lecture between each rally. Surely no one watches tennis who has no knowledge of the game. And, incidentally, everything the commentator says is so obvious.*

If you're a connoisseur of harsh words, consider this letter from M. Hodgkinson of Dartford in Kent (how appropriate) on the subject of Darts.

*I am compelled to write to complain about the staggering hopelessness of the commentators for the darts this Tuesday. Their counting is bad; six obvious mistakes were made on the late coverage Tuesday. An innocent Belgian Luc Mareel was in the space of two games called Lucky Mareel, Looky Mareel, Luck, Look, Luke and at one point Lofty! Mr Green observed 'I don't know what he said but it was in Belgian' – what? Mr Waddel described him as a 'Macbeth like character' and followed by saying that he, (Mareel) would be très heureux (pronounced tres huru) 'if this goes in' – indeed!*

*Mr Waddel noticed his 'lack of beer-gut' and said it was 'a credit to the game'.*

*The image of darts to the public of being a beer drinker's domain is being influenced less by the size of participants stomachs, than by the inarticulate, innumerate, pretentious banality of its commentary.*

## Sports on TV

Finally, in this section, a letter that is unsigned. All I know is that it comes from Ramsgate. Its message is clear and to the point.

*I am fed up with these selfish people who keep moaning about the sports commentators. I am blind and without them I would not be able to follow the many sports I enjoy! Like most blind people I like to lead a normal life, and prefer watching T.V. with my family than shutting myself away in another room just because I can't follow what is going on. Well done.*

# The Dartist

*Alan Bold*

He watches Eric Bristow on the box
And sees the treble twenties darting home.
He knows he's set to make his local team:
He also serves who only stands and chalks.

His moment comes, the tournament begins:
It's treble this, it's double this and that.
His pinkie's poised, he's looking really great,
He pushes home the darts like drawing pins.

His life has changed, his nights out with the lads
Are magic – he's heroic in their eyes.
He packs his job in for a higher prize:
His walls are weakened by a zillion thuds.

When his wife leaves he shrugs and shakes his head.
He much prefers to score three-in-a-bed.

*Sports on TV*

# Sumo Wrestlers

*James Kirkup*

If looks could kill,
These two hunks
Of sullen meat would long ago
Have eyed each other dead.

Bestowing on the fan-flocked air
Brief cascades of salt,
They stump slowly,
With studied boredom,
Into the ring of sand,
Huge flesh slopping,
Rumps and hams pocked and scarred
In black breechclouts.

Adjusting their bland bellies,
They arrange dainty hands
On the ground before them,
Crouch like grumpy toads.
But something tells them this
Is not the moment to engage.

They stretch up,
Tall in lacquered topknots,
And give each other long looks,
Contempt? No.
Intimidation? Perhaps.

Slowly lumber away
And leisurely return,

## Sumo Wrestlers

Spraying parabolas of tired salt
To purify the ring,
Propitiate the gods.

Crouched again, calm thighs
Spread, clash
Suddenly together
Push slap shove hook grunt heave
Buttressed against each other

Bare backsides cruppered
Black-belted bellies uddering
Paws groping for a girth-hold
Brute buttocks and bellies grappled
In shuddering embrace.

Till one is toppled,
Flopped like an avalanche,
Ten tons of rice-balls tumbling
Into a pleased ringside geisha's lap.

*Sports on TV*

# The Game's All About Clichés, Innit?

## Fritz Spiegl

**As the season begins, Fritz Spiegl gives a dazzling, virtuoso display of football parlance for the discerning amateur**

How did the game start?
*At a cracking pace.*
And then?
*It was good, old-fashioned end-to-end stuff.*
How did the player lose the ball?
*He was bundled off it.*
Yes, but *how?*
*Unceremoniously.*
And the other chap – where did he finish up?
*On the floor.*
In what position?
*Prone on his back.*
How did he leave the field?
*He was stretchered off.*
And then?
*Hospitalized.*
Will he be out of the game?
*Yes, sidelined.*
What did the referee do?
*He pointed to the spot.*
At once?
*Sorry. He had no hesitation in pointing to the spot.*
And the player who took the penalty, what did he do?
*He calmly stepped up.*
And then?
*He made no mistake.*
In other words . . . ?
*He gave the goalkeeper no chance.*
Until then, what had the goalie kept?
*A clean sheet.*
How must you then describe the goalkeeper?
*Hapless.*
And so, when Rovers scored, what did they do?
*They opened their account.*
Why did the goalkeeper come off his line?
*To narrow the angle.*
How would you describe the next goal?
*What a goal!*
And the save?
*What a save!*
Yes, but please describe its quality.
*World class.*
When did the goal come?
*Just before half time.*
Which is . . . ?
*The psychological moment.*
Which way were they playing?
*From left to right.*
And the others?
*From right to left, silly.*
Where are the goalposts?
*Away to our right.*
And the others?

## The Game's All About Clichés, Innit?

*Away to our left.*
Where were you sitting?
*None of your business, is it?*
How did the player break his leg?
*After a challenge.*
What kind of challenge?
*Sickening.*
What did the defender get before he was sent off?
*A talking to.*
And then?
*He took the long and lonely walk to the dressing room.*
After which he . . . ?
*Had an early bath, of course.*
How did his manager look?
*He looked pensive.*
The last-minute equalizer Rovers scored . . .
*Yes, it spared their blushes.*
And what happened to the game?
*It was snatched from the jaws of defeat.*
And when they then scored again?
*They went back in front.*
How surprised were you?
*It was a turn-up for the books*
And at the end . . .
*He blasted it high and wide.*
And . . . ?
*Not very handsome.*
He missed an open goal, I believe.
*Yes, gaping. It was a sitter.*
And the other side?
*They have it to do all over again.*
Where did the ball go when it failed to go in?
*Narrowly wide.*
How many kinds of foul are there?
*Three. Blatant, cynical and professional.*
What sort of stuff was it.
*Pulsating.*
What sort of a finish was it?
*A grandstand finish.*
And at the end, the referee . . . ?
*Blew up.*
So it was a draw. What did the managers say?
*We got a result.*

# *Just for Fun*

# Playing for Wales

*Max Boyce*

> I'll ne'er forget those childhood days
> E'en when the mem'ry fails
> I'll always fond remember
> Those times I played for Wales.

In the mining valleys in which I was brought up everybody has played for Wales; few, however, have actually pulled on the scarlet jersey and run on to Cardiff Arms Park, but we've all played at some time or other.

We had our own 'national stadiums' in streets and in back lanes and on bits of waste ground behind welfare halls, where rubbish bins became goalposts and tin sheets became corner flags.

They were multi-purpose grounds, for in the summer they became 'The Oval' and 'Lords' and other famous test-cricket grounds. The 'goalposts' became wickets, the tin sheets became the sightscreens and Clive Davies's father's garage became the Pavilion end.

One of my friends, Owen Phillips, was the finest 'street' opening bat I have ever seen. He used to draw the wickets with white chalk on the back door of his house. When you claimed you'd 'bowled' him he'd deny it, saying, 'There's no chalk on the ball!'

I'd never argue (he was bigger than me) with the result that before the 'out in the gardens' rule was introduced he was 'in' once for fourteen weeks. I forget how much he scored, but I know we lost. . . .

But it was Rugby we played most . . .

I'll always remember the first time I played for Wales – it was in Llywellyn Street, I was nine at the time and it was against England (it was always against England). I remember we had twenty-eight on our side and . . . three on their side. It wasn't fair but it was my ball!

I remember we won 406–12 in one of those games where you played four hours each way and only stopped when a ball went under a lorry. In that game I scored twenty-three tries before I was carried off injured: I was late tackled into touch three yards short of my anorak.

We went on to beat Ireland and Scotland – before three o'clock. We would have beaten France as well but Mel Thomas kicked the ball into Mrs Harries's garden and she wouldn't let us have it back. She was a funny woman (from Cardiff). We had her back though – we woke her tortoise up and gave it to this drunk and told him it was a pastie.

So then I'd run home and play in the back lane behind my house. I used to make rugby posts out of old kidney-bean sticks; for a ball I used to use an old fairy liquid bottle. I was the best kicker of a fairy liquid bottle in all Glamorgan. I could screw kick to touch and make the top come off. On thinking back, in all those times never once did we lose. We nearly did once: we were losing to England 36–3 with two minutes to go when – lucky – my mother called me for dinner.

*Just for Fun*

# The Village Cricket Match

*Ian McDonald*

The best way of relieving the strain of having nothing to do came in epic village cricket matches which sometimes lasted right through the day from early morning until nightfall. They were played on the rough village pasture. The outfield layout was littered with clots of dung.

I watched one of these big cricket matches once with Kaiser. He was in the village team. They were playing a side from the old village. It was a game hilariously, intensely, and fiercely contested. The day's casualties were high, several bruised heads and broken shins and three fractured noses, but the game seemed to let loose a surge of good humour in the villagers. There was one fight, between a visiting batsman and one of the home umpires, but this was soon over, with the umpire, chosen for his toughness, an easy winner, and the game continued smoothly after it.

Each team consisted of fifteen or sixteen men. I noticed that on Kaiser's side anyway the best batsmen opened the innings and then later, when the opponents could be supposed to have half-forgotten what they looked like, in again at number thirteen or fourteen they strode, wearing different caps. There were complaints, but never successful complaints, about this practice; it was the caps rather than the men who batted.

I gathered these caps were all-important in the game. The team which appeared with the most memorable caps was well on its way to triumph. The village team was pretty well unbeatable, for in its ranks, it boasted a green Trinidad XI cap. One day at the Oval a great star, as he walked in through a corridor of people applauding a brilliant century, had thrown his cap to a little boy from the village. He came home with it and sold it to the cricket team for five shillings. Now it starred in every game.

# The Village Cricket Match

In this particular match it made four appearances in the batting order and each of its scores was a highlight of the innings. Kaiser was one of those honoured with the green cap. He let me touch it and examine the treasured emblem on it, the Trinidad crest, the black-masted ships of Columbus in a blue harbour and in the background the trinity of green mountain peaks.

'Oh, God, I hope I score big,' Kaiser said fervently as he put it on to go in to bat.

After a nervous start he hit seventeen fiery runs. He hooked one ball into the casuarina tree which grew in the bush in front of Old Boss's hut; the game was held up twenty minutes while both teams searched the undergrowth; the ball was finally recovered from a patch of razor grass into which Kaiser, protesting, was made to go and where he emerged ball in hand but woebegone, slashed by the delicate, sharp, green blades. The next ball he lifted for another six and hit his mother's cow in the field adjoining; it began to moo disconsolately. In the midst of the cheers for such a fine hit, his mother rushed out into the playing field shouting angrily.

'You crazy or what, boy! Look what the hell you do now! You want to kill we cow or what, eh! Come out from dey an' see what I going gi' you here today!'

She advanced towards the pitch; Kaiser retreated from his wicket. The bowler took off his cap and fanned his face. The other fieldsman flopped down on the grass and took a rest. The two umpires conferred quickly and then told Kaiser's mother she must go. She refused.

'Le' me get am han' on that wotless chile an' I going beat him like I beat a donkey. You hear me cow, you hear it!' The cow was still mooing as if it had all the woes of the world on its back.

Confusion reigned. The umpires conferred again, but could reach no decision. The rest of the village team came streaming out on to the field. A babble of voices and a waving of arms began. In the middle of it all Kaiser's determined mother stood firm cursing.

'All you big men like baby or what? What you playing this dam

145

*Just for Fun*

foolish thing for? Why you don' go an' work, eh! You only was'ing you' time wid this chupid little ball an' piece of ol' wood. You' brain mus' be sof'ning fo' true. Look what he do me cow, eh! You hear it?' The cow was still mooing, distraughtly now.

At last they called Kaiser's father. He was in Ramlal's rumshop where he had gone for a rum. He was slightly drunk. He commanded his wife to go off the field when he heard the story.

'Woman, ge' off this fiel' here today,' he said ponderously, 'or I going well beat you. You hear me. Gawd, if you had Bra'man fo' you' son you would vex if he hit you' cow or what! The dam' cow not dead. Go, move, cle' the field, play, play!' he ended, flushed with triumph.

His wife went off crying. Play was resumed. The bowler swung his arms, glared at Kaiser, pounded down and delivered his stock ball, a fast full pitch. Kaiser swung hugely, missed, and was clean-bowled. The fieldsmen clapped the bowler. Kaiser walked away from his wicket, head bowed. As he came to the boundary edge his father caught hold of him and began to beat his ears mercilessly.

'Who you think you is, eh, firing shot at we cow like you mad? You don't know cow cos' money or what!'

Kaiser slipped through his arms and ran for his life, the green cap awry on his head; as he ran he straightened it proudly. The team scored 123 runs of which Kaiser's 17 was top score.

The score of 123 was too formidable for the opposing team. The village's star fast bowler, Burnly Hing, a Chinese-Indian who shared a hut with two brothers, who mended motor cars when he wasn't drunk, and who consumed more rum than anyone else in the village, really mowed down the visiting team. He took eight fair wickets and dismissed two other men with broken noses. His fierce slinging delivery was suspect and he was volubly accused of throwing the ball.

'Gawd Almighty!' the visiting captain said in an explosion of righteous despair. 'Gawd Almighty! What kin' of game this is.

# The Village Cricket Match

Gawd, man, me di'n' come here to pelt mango, oui! I never see a man pelt so. Eh, what you saying umpire?'

The umpires shook their heads sadly. The only consolation that the captain had was in scoring ten runs out of their small total of 44, and that ten was top score. Burnley Hing, in whose face lurked a thousand smiles of triumph, was hugely cheered. As he wiped his sweating face with a large silk handkerchief, he expressed himself.

'Where dat rum now, boy? I could drink a barrel o' rum here tonight!'

These matches, especially in the slack season when thirsts were so high, were profitable occasions for Ramlal, the richest man in the village. After the game both teams invaded his rumshop. Then the glum visitors recovered their spirits.

*Just for Fun*

# The Day I Ran for England

*Geraldine Kaye*

At the age of four I went in for the sister's race at my brother's school sports. I was not streetwise at the time and didn't really understand what a race was. There I was standing on a lawn with the other sisters and all round people were shouting 'Run' and 'Go to Daddy' and 'Not that way' and things like that. So I ran and I won. My success was probably because I was the largest competitor but nobody told me this. My prize was a small purple bag stuffed with needles and cottons for mending socks which I treasured for years. I came away with the conviction that I was a very good runner.

Being a total rabbit at all school games did not dispel this, though I had the wit to keep my conviction a secret. At netball I was, I suppose, fair but at all the small-ball games, such as hockey, lacrosse, tennis, cricket and rounders, I was hopeless. At the school where I stayed longest the headmistress had been a hockey international in her youth, or so it was rumoured, and we all spent an hour and a half daily in compulsory small-ball games. However, as I picked daisies on mid-off or shivered on the wing according to season, I clung to the notion that I could run fast and one day somebody would realize and give me a prize for it.

At eighteen I joined the Women's Royal Naval Service or 'Wrens' and was posted to the naval air station at Eastleigh near Southampton. I was a messenger and my duties mostly plodding round the airfield collecting the contents of out-trays and transferring them to in-trays somewhere else. It was boring but restful and I quite enjoyed it at the time.

One day the Gunnery Officer called for Wren volunteers to learn to shoot with a rifle. I volunteered with half a dozen others.

# The Day I Ran for England

The Gunnery Officer was exceptionally dishy for one thing. One evening we took ourselves to a Nissen hut which had a wooden bank covered with matting at our end and a set of targets at the other end and yards of peat in between. The Gunnery Officer demonstrated sighting and loading and firing our rifles and we lay down on the bank to try it out. I put five shots straight through the bulls-eye. I was astonished and so was everybody else.

The Gunnery Officer gave me another rifle and I did the same thing again. He was normally a phlegmatic fellow, but by this time he had begun to talk excitedly of my being a 'natural'. He even started planning a team of crack shot Wrens to compete all over the county. It was heady stuff. However, at this point the Goddess of Fluke deserted me and my next set of shots failed even to hit the target as did my next. The Gunnery Officer grew pale and silent. The Wren's team vanished like a mirage. After a second evening of failure and ignominy I allowed my place to be taken by the more talented. Shooting, like small-ball games, was not for me.

Two years later I went up to university and in the first week of term signed up for a variety of student clubs and activities. One of these was rowing. We took ourselves to Morden on the Thames on Wednesday and Saturday afternoons and practised initially in a specially fitted boatshed. I was spotted as likely material and soon found myself in a team of four rowing up and down the river in very brief shorts. There was talk of rowing for the university and getting a *purple*. Everybody has heard of Oxford and Cambridge blues which are guaranteed to smooth any future career paths. Nobody has heard of London University's purples which are also awarded for sport but somehow lack cachet. Rowing had the disadvantage that it rendered me exhausted to the point of insensibility for Wednesday and Saturday evenings and seriously interfered with my social life, let alone my study. But the crucial test was an unusually cold winter. As I dipped my flat-bladed oar into the water it rounded out like a chopstick with ice in an instant and was exceedingly

*Just for Fun*

heavy. Besides, the possibility of capsizing was daunting and I gave up on rowing and the purple.

The following spring the noticeboard invited student volunteers to work for eight weeks of the summer vacation on the Youth Railway in Yugoslavia to run from Samac to Sarajevo, a distance of sixty miles. I volunteered. I nearly didn't get there. I had to be vaccinated. My mother had strong anti-vaccination views and I had never been done as a baby. I had a very violent reaction, ran a temperature of 105 degrees and was quite delirious. However, I recovered in time to get myself and my rucksack on the train along with two hundred others.

Peace was still relatively recent and bombing had destroyed much of Europe including its railway tracks, and I suppose a train full of students had a low priority. At any rate it took five days to get from Dover to Belgrade. At intervals we were unloaded and fed. I remember a large bowl of gruel at Innsbruck for instance, but we spent long days and nights stuck in sidings. The first night you spread your sleeping-bag on a station platform with a hundred others you don't sleep much, but the second night you sleep as if to the manner born.

Finally we arrived at our camp in Bosnia, already a going concern. The whole project was both idealistic and left-wing and we solemnly called each other 'comrade'. We slept in large wooden huts but instead of two-tier bunks there were two-tier continuous shelves with sleepers in serried ranks. There was a roofed dining area and a rudimentary latrine and wash block across a maize field. Our camp cook and our camp leader had both been in the International Brigade which had fought in the Spanish Civil War ten years previously. They seemed very heroic to the rest of us.

We breakfasted on black bread and ersatz coffee and started work at six o'clock. Our task was building an embankment to carry the railway across the wooded valley where we were camped. The technique was simple. You broke the earth with a pick, shovelled it into a barrow, pushed the barrow up a ramp, tipped it out and started the process over again. An embankment

# The Day I Ran for England

of yellow earth already snaked its way across the green valley. The Greeks in the next camp were dynamiting a tunnel through the adjoining mountain at considerable risk to life and limb. At night we still found the energy to meet up and dance round bonfires with them. Ronald Searle came and drew us.

Somebody asked for volunteers to run in some forthcoming international sports at Belgrade and I volunteered. I ran a few heats alongside other would-be competitors and was duly selected. The enthusiast in charge of us reckoned himself expert and subjected me to a week of intensive training. I was so stiff after two days I could hardly walk. However, we set off for Belgrade and the international camp. It was huge and exceedingly crowded. Bodies sleeping on continuous shelves could always be bunched up to accommodate a few more and they were. The latrines were deep pits five feet by twenty with loose planks laid at precarious intervals. The stink was prodigious and visits at night quite out of the question. Fortunately my training rendered me unconscious for all the hours of darkness.

On the great day I was lined up with three other women, one Czech, one Canadian and one Hungarian. 'Don't forget you're running for England,' my trainer said fervently. The whistle blew. I ran. The Czech won. I'm not sure whether I was second or third but I know I wasn't last. However, it was the end of my athletic career.

One of the advantages of being grown-up is that you don't have to do things unless you're good at them and want to. Now and then I tell my children how I once ran for England but they never seem that impressed. However, I have great hopes it will go down big with my granddaughter.

# Activities

## *Football Crazy*

### Background notes

Tony Drake teaches in an Oxfordshire school. He has written several novels for young people including *There will be a Next Time, Look through any Window* and *Playing it Right*, a cricketing story. He explains the background to *The Trial*:

> *The Trial* comes from a longer, unfinished story about Colin, a talented footballer, who is taken from the local league to play as a part-time professional for the local 3rd Division side. The reason why the story is – as yet – unfinished is that I have not been able to resolve the problem of what happens to Colin at United.
>
> I have a number of reasons for wanting to write this story. In all the years that I have followed, played and coached football, I have seen a complete change in the attitude towards black players. And yet there is still an intolerable level of racism in the game, and not just on the terraces. We may lose sight of this now that there are so many black players in the British game, but there are still lots of things happening that make me very angry.
>
> And that brings me to the other main reason for wanting to write this story. Football – and all sport – can make me feel angry and sad, elated and utterly miserable. Why is this? It's only a game, isn't it? And there are lots more important things than *games*, aren't there? Of course there are, but you just try telling me that when I've just missed an open goal or been bowled for a duck ...

Gareth Owen is the author of two books of poems for young people, *Salford Road* and *Song of the City* (in which *The Commentator* appears) and several novels, including *The Final Test*, a story about the friendship between two boys both of whom are passionately fond of cricket.

*A Soccer Star Narrowly Missed* is from a collection of sporting limericks, *There was a young fellow called Glover*, edited by Simon Barnes.

Activities

*World Cup* by Paul Higgins is from *Madtail, Miniwhale and Other Shape Poems* chosen by Wes Magee.

Michael Rosen is a well-known children's poet. His books include *Mind Your Own Business, Wouldn't You Like to Know* and, together with Roger McGough, *You Tell Me*.

Joanna White is a pupil at Riverside School, Thamesmead. She wrote *Dad* in memory of the 95 people who died at Hillsborough in March 1989, when they were crushed against the perimeter fencing at the F.A. Cup semi-final between Liverpool and Nottingham Forest.

Barry Hines is the son of a miner. When he left school, he played football for Barnsley and did various jobs before training as a P.E. teacher. He taught for two years in a London comprehensive school and then became a full-time writer. His novels include *The Blinder*, the story of Lennie Hawk, a promising young footballer, and *A Kestrel For a Knave*, which was turned into the highly successful film, *Kes*.

Michael Parkinson, the journalist and TV personality, is a lifelong football fan. *Clakker May* is from his book *Football Daft*.

Brian Glanville works as a journalist on *The Sunday Times*. He is one of Britain's leading football writers and he scripted and helped to edit *Goal*, the award-winning documentary film on the 1966 World Cup. He has written many books about football, including the novels *The Rise of Gerry Logan* and *Goalkeepers are Different*. A collection of his sports stories *Goalkeepers are Crazy* is available in the Longman Imprint series.

*The Ref's a Woman!* is an article which appeared in *The Independent* on Friday 10th February 1989.

## The Trial

### Pair Work

1  What are Colin's feelings, before, during and after the match? Draw a chart or a diagram showing what Colin's feelings are.
2  By writing in the first person, Tony Drake helps us to see the events through Colin's eyes. Try rewriting a section of the story in the third person. Discuss what difference it makes.
3  Read Tony Drake's background note. Are there any hints in the story so far that Colin is black? What do you think are the sort of things that make Tony Drake angry? Suggest ways that he might continue the story.

## Activities

**Written assignments**

1   How would you continue Tony Drake's story? Write either the next chapter of the story or another story describing one of Colin's experiences as a part-time professional. Try to write in the same style as Tony Drake does.
2   Think about any trials or important matches you have taken part in, not necessarily football matches. Use one as the starting point and write either a story or an autobiographical account based on your experiences. Try, as Tony Drake does, to let the reader know the emotions you felt before, during and after the trial.

## The Commentator

**Pair work**

1   Take it in turns to read Gareth Owen's poem aloud, as if a sports commentator was speaking. Plan your reading carefully, varying your pace and pitch as appropriate at the more eventful moments in the story. Tape-record your commentaries and play them back to the rest of the class. Whose commentary works best? Discuss why.
2   Why do you think Gareth Owen chose to write his story as a poem in the form of a sports commentary? Do you think the story could have been written in a different way, using either a different verse form or as a piece of prose? If so, do you think it would have been as effective? Give your reasons.
3   In your pairs, produce a chart showing how during the course of the poem, Gareth Owen uses the language of sports commentary to:
*a)* set the scene
*b)* describe a fast piece of action
*c)* comment on the player's skill
*d)* describe an unusual and unexpected turn of events
*e)* tell the listener about the crowd's reactions.
4   Pick out some uses of language in the poem which are typical of a spoken commentary rather than a written report, e.g. The use of 'And' at the start of a new utterance; the repetition of statements to emphasize key developments in the action; the use of short phrases rather than complete sentence units to describe a quick series of events. Find examples of such features. What other language features can you find that are more typical of a sports commentary than of written Standard English?

## Activities

**Written assignments**

1 Use Gareth Owen's poem as a model and write a similar poem in which you use the form of a sports commentary to describe an incident involving a teenager and an adult, for example in a classroom, a supermarket, a swimming baths or a park. Here is the start of such a poem:

>Good afternoon and welcome,
>This is Debra Gould your commentator
>Welcoming you to this geography lesson
>Between 5X and Mr Allsop
>Being held in Room 53 A
>At Sir George Markly Comprehensive School...

2 Write a report of the game described in *The Commentator* for a newspaper of your choice. Use the style appropriate for that newspaper.

## World Cup

**Pair work**

1 Discuss how Paul Higgins has created a collage poem about the World Cup by selecting headlines and arranging them to form the shape of the World Cup trophy.

Study the poem carefully and discuss the words and phrases that he has chosen. What overall impression of the World Cup does his poem create? How effective do you think it is?

2 Work together to produce a collage poem of your own that forms the shape of a sports trophy or a piece of sporting equipment. For example, you could produce a collage poem about Wimbledon in the shape of the plate awarded to the Ladies' singles champion or in the shape of a tennis racket. You could also create a poem about rugby in the shape of a rugby ball.

Choose your words and headlines carefully, then form groups with other pairs and explain why you chose these particular words and phrases.

## Unfair

**Group work**

1 In mixed groups, discuss Michael Rosen's poem. Have the girls in your group had any similar experiences? Should girls who are good

# Activities

enough be allowed to play in a school's football team? What are the arguments for and against them being allowed to do so?

2  Find out what opportunities there are to play women's football in your area. How do these compare with the opportunities for boys to play football? List what you think schools, colleges, local councils and local clubs should do to provide more opportunities for women to play football.

### Written assignments

1  Write an article for a teenage magazine about women's football and what needs to be done to improve facilities and opportunities for women to play football in your area.

2  Write a poem in a similar style to Michael Rosen's about a game in which Lizzie *does* play.

## The Big Match

### Group work

1  What do you learn from Barry Hines's autobiographical story about the part football played in his life as a teenager? Why does he call it *The Big Match*?

2  What were the most important lessons Barry Hines learnt from the experience of playing for the England Schools team? How was Barry Hines and his working-class friends' attitude to football different from the attitudes of the people at his Grammar School and of the public school boys he met at the England Schools trial?

### Written assignment

Imagine one of the public school boys writes a letter to a friend about the trials in Cambridge. Write an extract from the letter in which he describes and comments on the young Hines.

## Clakker May

### Group work

1  Talk about what happens in Michael Parkinson's story *Clakker May*. Which parts of the story did you find amusing? The humour is at Clakker's expense. Does that matter?

Activities

2  Discuss the structure and style of the story:
a) What is the purpose of the introductory paragraph? How is its style different from the style of the rest of the story? What difference would it make if it was omitted and the story began at the start of the second paragraph?
b) The narrative is written in Standard English but when the characters speak Michael Parkinson imitates their dialect and accents. What effect does this have? What difference would it make to the story if he had not imitated the characters' dialect and accent or, alternatively, if the whole story had been written in dialect?

## I Didn't Do Nothing

### Group work

1  Discuss Brian Glanville's use of the narrator's voice in *I Didn't Do Nothing* to convey the referee's character. What impression do you get of the referee from what he says? What mental picture do you form of him?
2  Discuss the way the referee handled Jack Benbow. Why did Benbow hit him? At the end of the story where do your sympathies lie – with Benbow or with the referee?

### Written assignments

1  Write two short newspaper articles that appeared on the day Jackie Benbow received his *sine die* suspension, one for a quality paper, with a headline such as 'Talented Benbow gets sine die suspension', one for a popular paper with a headline such as: 'BENBOW BANNED'.
2  Compare the three stories – *The Trial, Clakker May* and *I Didn't Do Nothing*. Comment on the structure and style of the stories and the narrative techniques which the authors use.

## The Ref's a Woman!

### Pair work

1  Discuss the prejudice which Cayline Vincent encounters, as a woman trying to establish herself as a rugby league referee. Why is there such prejudice? Is it confined to rugby league? What is the best way to counter such prejudice?

Activities

2   Role play a scene in which a TV sports reporter interviews Cayline Vincent asking her why she took up refereeing and about the problems and prejudices she has encountered. Before you begin, draw up a list of questions for the interviewer to ask and study the article carefully, so that the answers Cayline Vincent gives are based on what the article tells you.

# *Sports in School*

## Background notes

Adèle Geras was born in Jerusalem and brought up in England. After university, she worked as a professional singer and then as a teacher and travelled widely. She now lives in Manchester and writes full time. Her books for young people include *The Green Behind the Glass*, a collection of love stories, and *Letters of Fire* a collection of unsettling tales.

Roger Mills' account of his games lessons is from *A Comprehensive Education*, published by Centreprise.

David Williams lives in Northumberland. He has written a number of plays which have been broadcast in schools radio programmes. *Skivers* was specially written for this anthology.

John Foster lives in Abingdon, Oxfordshire. He has edited many anthologies for schools, including a popular Oxford poetry series for juniors. He likes all kinds of sport. He is a keen skier and supports Carlisle United.

Jan Mark is a leading children's writer. She trained as a teacher and taught English and Art for six years before embarking on her writing career. Her books have won several literary awards including the Carnegie Medal.

Brian Keaney grew up in the East End of London and was a teacher before becoming a full-time writer. *Aliens* is from a book of autobiographical short stories *Don't Hang About* published by Oxford University Press.

Dorian Wood is a former games teacher, who now teaches history in a girls' independent school. The article first appeared in the magazine *Teacher's Weekly* in October 1988.

Judith Nicholls has written two collections of poems for children – *Magic Mirror* and *Midnight Forest*. She has also edited a book of poems

Activities

with a conservation theme *What on Earth . . . ?* The poem *Miss Willis P.E.* was specially written for this collection.

Lesley Davies's family kept moving when she was a child, so she attended several schools. She tells the story of 'the first part of my crazy life' in *Lesley's Life* (Longman Knockouts).

## The Screams of the Damned

### Pair work

1  Talk about why the girl in Adèle Geras's story is 'relieved to be done with games'. What do you think she dislikes more – games in the summer or games in the winter?
2  What impression do you get of the girl in Adèle Geras's story from the way she writes about games and her attitude towards them? Say what sort of person you think she is.
3  A sporty type at the same school, who enjoys games 'hugely' would no doubt have written about games in a very different way. Draw up a list of the points in favour of the games played:
*a)* in the winter
*b)* in the summer
that she would have included.

### Written assignment

Try writing Adèle Geras's story from the viewpoint of a girl who hates being cooped up in the library and longs to be out on the gamesfield. Present the points on what she likes about summer games as a list. Then write about what she likes about winter games as a piece of continuous prose. Write in the present tense, as Adèle Geras does.

## That Showed 'Em

### Group work

1  Talk about Roger Mills's experience of games at his school. How far is his attitude to games the same as the girl in Adèle Geras's story?
2  Discuss the incident that ended Roger's football career. Share memories of any incidents that have happened to you during P.E. and games lessons.
3  Talk about what you do in P.E. and games lessons. List what you enjoy and what you dislike about your P.E. lessons. If you could change

## Activities

P.E. lessons, how would you make them different? Keep notes of your discussion to use when drafting your written assignment.

### Written assignment

Write about your P.E. and games lessons in the way that Roger Mills has written about his. Make it clear to the reader how much you enjoy them, dislike them or are indifferent to them. Include a detailed account of one incident that reflects why you feel the way you do about P.E. and games.

### Skivers/After Sports Day

#### Pair work and group work

1  Why do Claire and Paula decide to skive off? What is your opinion of their behaviour? Do you despise them for doing so or sympathize with them, because they are being forced to do something they do not want to do?

2  What do you learn about Claire's and Paula's attitude to sport from their conversation while they are having coffee? What else do you learn about them?

3  How does Paula's attitude differ from Claire's at the end of the play when she realizes what has happened? If you had been in their situation, what would you have done – tried to bluff it out, gone and owned up, or run off and postponed the inevitable showdown with Miss Dunn?

4  What do you think will happen when the truth is discovered?

*a)* Role play a scene in which Helen Clark finally gets Miss Dunn to listen to what she has to say.

*b)* Role play a scene in which Miss Dunn confronts Claire and Paula. What does she say to them? Does she punish them in any way?

*c)* Role play a scene later that week in which some other girls gossip about what Claire and Paula did. Show the different attitudes the girls might take, some of them thinking it a great laugh, while others are thoroughly disapproving, branding them as cheats.

5  Read John Foster's poem *After Sports Day*. Talk about the issues it raises.

*a)* Do parents and teachers place too much emphasis on winning and the winners in school sports?

*b)* What are the arguments people use to support splitting school year groups into houses and organizing house competitions at events such as

## Activities

school sports? Do you think such competitions are a good idea? Should pressure be put on everybody to take part?

6 Prepare either a tape-recording or a presentation of the play. Before you start, try to 'get inside' the characters of Claire, Paula and Helen by each taking one of them and imagining what she is like in other situations. For example, what is her home like? How many people are there in her family? What are her hobbies and interests? Is she good at her schoolwork? What are her ambitions? Get one of the group to think about Miss Dunn in a similar way. Then compare your ideas about their characters.

When you have thought carefully about each of the characters, hold several rehearsals, reading the play through and thinking about how you are going to speak your lines, before making the tape-recording or presenting a reading of the play.

### Written assignments

1 Write two short accounts of the events described in *Skivers* in the form of diary entries, one describing what happened from either Claire's or Paula's point of view, the other describing the events from either Helen's or Miss Dunn's point of view.

2 Write a short playscript, a short story or an article for a school magazine based around your experiences of, and views on, sports days and inter-house sports competitions.

## Aliens

### Group work

1 What do you learn about Brian Keaney and his attitude to rugby from *Aliens*? Why did he dislike rugby so much? Why did his friend Kevin like rugby? What is your view of rugby as a sport?

2 Discuss what happens in the second half of the story.

*a)* Why is Brian's enjoyment of rugby so short-lived?

*b)* Focus on the final two paragraphs.

What conclusion does Brian Keaney draw about the sort of people who are likely to enjoy rugby? Discuss what he says about the killer instinct.

### Written assignment

Discuss with a partner how Brian Keaney uses his daydreams to reinforce the view of rugby that he puts across in this story. Then, on

## Activities

your own, use the daydream section of the story as a model and write a similar description of another sporting activity, as it might be reported by a planetary ecologist. Then, form groups and discuss each other's reports. Decide whose works best and why. Finally, redraft your report for your folder.

## Feet

### Group work

1  Work in groups of three. Imagine the final has just ended. Each take one of the three main characters: Jane, Collier and Carson, Write down what she/he is thinking at that point. Then, form larger groups and discuss what you have written.
2  What impression do you get of Jane from the way she tells the story? Write down your ideas about Jane and pick out evidence from the story to support your views.
3  In one or two sentences, sum up what the story is about. Talk about how Jan Mark uses the tennis competition as a setting for the story. Why does she involve Jane as the umpire, rather than as a competitor or as a spectator?
4  Why is the story called *Feet*? Find all the references to feet that occur in the story. Suggest alternative titles. Which alternative title is best? Say why.

### Written assignments

1  Use the notes you made while discussing the four questions above and write about Jan Mark's story *Feet*. Explain what the story is about, your response to it and comment on the style and the techniques the author uses to achieve her purpose.
2  Write a story about a person's feelings or relationships which, like *Feet*, is set against the background of a sports event or a games lesson.

## Games Should Not Be Compulsory

### Group work

1  According to Dorian Wood, how have attitudes to team games changed both in school and society? In your experience, is it true that

# Activities

'a schoolboy learns meanness and intolerance as an integral part of his sport'?
2  What is Dorian Wood's view of the proliferation of non-team activities?
3  According to Dorian Wood, what would be the advantages to a school, both educationally and financially, of making games a voluntary option?
4  What do you think of Dorian Wood's views? What other arguments are sometimes put forward to support the abolition of compulsory games? What arguments are used to support compulsory P.E. and games in schools? Make notes of the arguments that are put forward. Then, organize a formal debate: 'This house believes that it is important for all students to do P.E. and games throughout their school careers.'

### Written assignment

Write an article for a magazine Talkback column in response to Dorian Wood's article stating your views on whether or not games should be compulsory. As well as stating your arguments and giving your reasons for them, state what other people's arguments are and say why you disagree with them.

## Miss Willis, P.E.

### Pair work

1  What impression of Miss Willis do you get from reading Judith Nicholls' poem? Explain why, picking out details and any words and phrases in the poem which helped you to form your impression of her.
2  Talk about the structure of the poem. What is the different focus of each of the three verses?

### Written assignment

Write a poem like *Miss Willis, P.E.* in which you describe a person who is involved in sport – for example, a football coach, a judo instructor, a referee or another P.E. teacher. Your poem could be based on your observations of several different characters rather than one particular person. Then, write a commentary on Judith Nicholls' poem, referring to its purpose, style and structure, and a similar commentary on your own poem.

Activities

# *Practice makes Perfect*

## Background notes

James Kirkup was born in 1923 and educated at South Shields High School and Durham University. He now lives in Japan and has worked as a professor of English at several far eastern universities. He is a prolific writer and in addition to collections of poetry has written travel books, novels, plays and an account of his childhood, *The Only Child*.

*Practice makes Perfect* is from an autobiography of Daley Thompson, *One is My Lucky Number*, which was published in 1980. Like many autobiographies of sporting personalities, it was written by a 'ghost writer'. Daley Thompson supplied all the information about his life, but the final text of the book was produced by a professional writer.

*A Life in the Day of Joanne Conway* appeared in *The Sunday Times* magazine section on January 15th 1989. The article reads as if Joanne Conway wrote it. In fact, it is based on an interview with Joanne Conway and was composed by a journalist, Jenny Woolf.

The account of Matthew Bridgeman's training schedule appeared in the September 1988 issue of *Today's Runner*.

James Berry was born in Jamaica and has lived in England since 1948. He has published several collections of his own poetry and edited several other collections including *Bluefoot Traveller* and *News for Babylon*, two volumes of West Indian-British poetry. He has also written a prize-winning collection of short stories for young people, *A Thief in the Village*.

## High Dive

### Pair work

1  Work with a partner. Go through the poem section by section and discuss how James Kirkup tries to convey the artistry, skill and beauty of the dive. Which part of the poem do you find most effective? Say why.

2  Each prepare a reading of the poem. Whose reading works best? Why?

### Written assignment

Find a picture of a sportsperson in action, e.g. a javelin thrower about to throw, an archer about to fire, a golfer or a cricketer who has just

Activities

completed a stroke. Write a poem, similar to James Kirkup's, describing the action, the artistry and skill involved in the image.

## Practice Makes Perfect

### Group work

1  Discuss what you learn about Daley Thompson's training schedule and what Daley Thompson says about his trainer. What do you learn from the article about the relationship between a top athlete and his coach?
2  How and why does Daley Thompson's training schedule differ from that of a middle-distance runner? If you had to choose, whose schedule would you prefer – Daley Thompson's or a middle-distance runner's? Report your group's views in a class discussion.
3  On your own, go through the article as if you are a sub-editor and put in sub-headings to show the main topics. Then, in your groups, discuss where you have put the headings and why.

## A Life in the Day of Joanne Conway

### Group work

1  Think about Joanne Conway's life-style. Working on your own, list what you see as its good points and bad points. What sort of sacrifices has she had to make in her search for sporting success? If you were Joanne Conway, would you have been prepared to make those sacrifices? Share your views in a group discussion.
2  In groups, discuss the effects that Joanne's skating career have had on other members of her family. If one member of a family has a particular talent, how far should other members of the family be prepared to make sacrifices in order to give her/him the opportunity to develop that talent?
3  Discuss what you learn from the article about the part a sports psychologist may play in the life of an international skater. How important is mental strength to success in competition? Do you think it can be developed in the same way that physical skills can be learned?

### Written assignments

1  Interview someone who is a keen sportsperson about their training and practice. Prepare your questions carefully and either tape-record

## Activities

or make detailed notes of their answers. Then, ghost-write an article describing how they train or practise. Write the article in the first person in the way that a professional ghost-writer would.

2  Imagine that a magazine editor wants to include either the piece about Daley Thompson or the piece about Joanne Conway in her magazine, but that space available in the magazine is very tight. Choose one of the articles. Work with a partner and decide how you would cut the article to reduce it to about one-third of its original length.

## Lean lesson

### Pair work

1  Discuss why Matthew Bridgeman took up training. What effect has it had on him and his life? Why does he enjoy it?

2  What similarities and differences are there between the training schedule of an amateur, such as Matthew, and those of champions, such as Joanne Conway and Daley Thompson?

3  Imagine that one of you is Matthew and the other is a friend of his who is thinking of taking up running. Improvise the conversation in which Matthew talks enthusiastically about running and tries to persuade his friend to take it up.

### Written assignments

1  Write an autobiographical article like Matthew Bridgeman's describing how you first became interested in a particular sport and how you organize your training and practice.

2  Alternatively, write an article from the viewpoint of someone who heartily dislikes sport, and who cannot see the point of people becoming obsessed with training routines and physical fitness.

## Boxer Man In-a-Skippin' Workout

### Pair work

1  What impression of the skipping boxer does James Berry convey in his poem? Pick out the words and phrases he uses to achieve this.

2  Talk about the use James Berry makes of rhythm in this poem. How does this rhythm support the image created by the language. With your partner practise reading the poem aloud in order to capture its rhythm.

Activities

3   The poem is written in West Indian dialect rather than standard English. Why do you think James Berry chose to use this dialect rather than Standard English. Try to rewrite one of the verses in Standard English. What difference does it make?

## *Track and field*

### Background notes

*To James* is by an American writer Frank Horne.
*Raymond's run* is from Toni Cade Bambara's collection of short stories *Gorilla my Love* published by The Women's Press.

Mick Gowar lives in Cambridge. He has published three collections of poems for young people – *Swings and Roundabouts, So Far so Good* and *Live Album.*

Peter Carter is the author of several books for teenagers including *Under Goliath. The High Jump Competition* is from his novel *Bury the Dead*, the story of a talented young East German athlete, whose life is disrupted when an Uncle reappears and long-kept family secrets, to do with the horrors of Germany's past, are revealed.

Daved Bateson lives in New South Wales, Australia. *A Girl Called Golden* was specially written for this anthology.

Bill Boyle is a freelance journalist who lives in Cheshire. The article on the 1988 Paralympic Games was specially written for this anthology.

### To James

Pair work

Like many poems, this poem can be interpreted both literally and metaphorically. What is your response to the poem? Discuss different ways of reading and interpreting it.

### Raymond's Run

Pair work

1   Why is the story called, *Raymond's Run*? Do you think it is an appropriate title? Suggest some alternative titles.

## Activities

2 What impression do you get of the narrator. What sort of girl is she? Talk about the part running plays in her life. Do you think she and Gretchen will become friends? Explain why.
3 Discuss the conversational style in which *Raymond's Run* is written. Compare the way the story is narrated in *Raymond's Run* with the way in which other stories in this anthology are narrated, e.g. Jan Mark's *Feet* and Brian Keaney's *Aliens*.

### Written assignment

Work in pairs. Imagine that the local newspaper decides to run an article profiling the girl in *Raymond's Run* and predicting a bright future for her. Role play an interview between a reporter and Hazel. Then write a profile of her, describing how she trains, her successes so far and her hopes and ambitions.

## The Hero

### Group work

1 What do you think is the relationship between the boy and the man in the hospital? What is the boy's attitude towards the man? Is he the boy's hero? Suggest what the boy is thinking while the man is talking.
2 What impression do you get of the man from the way he speaks? Choose two or three words to describe him, then discuss the words you chose and why.
3 Talk about what the man says. What do you think of his attitude? If you had been in the man's position, with his talent, what choices would you have made?
4 What do you think is the poet's attitude towards the man? Do you think he approves of, disapproves of or is indifferent to the man's actions and attitudes? Say why.
5 Discuss the use of drugs to improve sporting performances. What action should be taken if a person is found to have used drugs? Talk about the treatment Ben Johnson received after he was tested positive following his win in the 1988 Olympic Games 100 metres. Do you think he has been made a scapegoat?

Activities

## The High Jump Competition

### Group work

1  Talk about how Peter Carter describes the pressures and tensions of a competition by letting the reader see into Erika's mind. How does Erika's mood change during and after the competition? Draw a chart or a diagram listing the events and showing Erika's emotions and changes of mood.
2  What is your final impression of Erika? Each write a thumb-nail sketch of her character. Then, in groups, discuss what you have written.
3  Talk about scruples. Was it wrong of Erika's coach to psych her up in the way she did? Why does the coach ask Erika to promise not to repeat their conversation? How do Erika's feelings about scruples alter after the presentation ceremony?
4  Peter Carter describes the events in *The High Jump Competiton* from Erika's point of view. How might they have been described differently by Karen Bloxen? Each write two or three paragraphs describing Karen's thoughts and feelings at one particular point in the story. Then, compare and discuss what you have written.

### Written assignment

Write the diary entry that Karen might have written that night, as she reflected on the events described in *The High Jump Competition*.

Write a story about a young competitor who has to make a difficult decision when faced with the choice of whether or not to be unscrupulous in order to win.

## A Girl Called Golden

### Group work

1  Work in groups of four and prepare a presentation reading of the poem.
2  Talk about how David Bateson uses the poem to celebrate Betty Cuthbert's achievement.
3  Discuss the questions David Bateson raises in the first two verses. How would you answer them? In your opinion what is it that motivates some people to dedicate themselves to trying to become champions?

Activities

**Written assignment**

Write a poem about a sporting hero in which you aim to celebrate her/his achievements in a similar way to the way that David Bateson celebrates Betty Cuthbert's achievements in *A Girl Called Golden*.

## The Eighth Paralympic Games, Seoul 1988

**Pair work**

1   Bill Boyle's article is a mixture of facts and opinions. Work with a partner and draw up two lists, one of the facts given in the article, the other of the opinions.
2   Talk about the way Bill Boyle stresses the contrasts between the 1988 Paralympic Games and the 1988 Olympic Games. What do you think of his views?
3   Discuss the language that Bill Boyle uses to put across his point of view. What is the effect of his use of terms, such as *squalid memories* and *pampered 'stars'*? Find other examples of his use of emotive language to influence the reader and to reinforce his viewpoint.
4   How much coverage are sports for the disabled given in the media? Do you think that sports editors should ensure that sports for the disabled are given more coverage on TV and in newspapers? Why do you think they are not given more coverage? Share your views in a class discussion.

## *But Is It sport?*

### Background notes

Irvin Ashkenazy is an American writer. His story *Pop's Boy* reveals some of the seamier features of professional boxing.

*Who Killed Davey Moore?* was written in 1964 by the folk singer Bob Dylan following the tragic death of Davey Moore after a boxing bout.

*Glove me Tender* is from an article entitled *Raging Belles* which appeared in *Sky* magazine in September 1988.

K. M. Peyton is a prizewinning writer of children's books including the *Flambards* trilogy, *Prove Yourself a Hero* and *A Midsummer Night's*

Activities

*Death*. She is a sailor and a keen rider. *A-hunting I Will Go, Without Shame* appeared in *The Guardian*.

Sam Ramsamy is executive chair of SA Non-Racial Olympic Committee, campaigning for South Africa's exclusion from international sport. *Moral Rules to Every Game* appeared in *The Independent* in August 1989 shortly after the annoucement of a rebel cricket tour to South Africa of England players captained by Mike Gatting.

Raymond Wilson lives in Henley, Oxfordshire. He has edited and contributed to many books of poems for young people, such as *Nine O'clock Bell*, a collection of poems about school. *The Progress of Sport* was specially written for this anthology.

## Pop's Boy

### Group work

1 Discuss the ending of the story. Did the final twists come as a surprise? Look back through the story. What clues does the author leave for the reader so that the ending can be seen to tie in with the rest of the story?
2 Talk about Pop. Suggest what must have been going through his mind as he watched the narrator's fight with Billy Terry. Why did he pay the narrator 300 dollars instead of 130 dollars?
3 What impression does the story give of the world of professional boxing? What do you think of the way Billy Terry fights and of the narrator's response? If someone fouls you, is it all right to foul them back?

## Who Killed Davey Moore?

### Group work

1 Talk about each of the six people featured in the poem in turn. Discuss the arguments each uses to deny responsibility for the death. Whose arguments do you find convincing?
2 Either tape-record or present a reading of the poem.
3 Role play a TV discussion on the subject of whether boxing should be banned. Make sure the panel includes people with a cross-section of differing views.

Activities

## Glove me Tender

### Group work

1 What do you learn from the article about Sue Atkins' and Karen Hope's reasons for boxing? Why do they like it?
2 Joe Lewis says 'Physiologically and psychologically women are not made for boxing.' Do you agree? Are you for or against women's boxing?
3 Should there be opportunities for women to participate in all sports or are there certain sports, such as boxing, which are unsuitable for women? What are your views, for example, on women's wrestling?

### Written assignment

Write an essay expressing your views about boxing as a sport.

## A-hunting I Will Go, Without Shame

### Group work

1 Kathleen Peyton admits that allowing the fox to be killed by a pack of hounds is cruel. What arguments does she use to make us think again before condemning it outright? Did she manage to persuade you to think again about fox-hunting?
2 What are your views on other blood sports, such as hare-coursing? What do you think of shooting birds as a sport? Is it right to rear birds specially so that people can shoot them? What do you think of fishing? Share your views about hunting, shooting and fishing in a group discussion.

### Written assignments

1 Write a letter to a newspaper or an article, similar to Kathleen Peyton's article, in which you reply to the arguments she puts forward and state your views on hunting as a sport.
2 Write an essay expressing your views about man's use of animals in sports. In addition to writing about hunting, shooting and fishing, include your views on sports such as greyhound racing, horse sports, pigeon-fancying and banned sports, such as cock-fighting and dog-fighting.

Activities

## Moral Rules to Every Game

Group work

1 Discuss Sam Ramsamy's views. On what grounds does he argue that international sports players should not play in South Africa and that South African teams should be excluded from international sport?
2 Work in groups of three. Role play a TV discussion. One person should act as chair, while the other two take opposing views in response to the views Sam Ramsamy puts forward in his article.
3 Organize a formal debate on the motion:
'This house believes that all sports players should support the boycott of playing in South Africa and against South African teams'.

Written assignment

Write a letter to a sports personality who has declared her/his intention to take part in a rebel tour of South Africa, saying why you support or disapprove of her/his decision.

## The Progress of Sport

Pair work

1 Go through the poem section by section, discussing what Raymond Wilson says. Which section do you think is most effective? Say why.
2 Prepare a reading of the poem, together with a short commentary explaining your response to it.
3 Why is the poem called *The Progress of Sport*? Write a short paragraph summarizing the views Raymond Wilson puts forward in the poem. Do you share his view that attitudes to sport have changed radically in recent years?

# *Sport on TV*

## Background notes

*Points of view* is a selection of letters sent in to the BBC TV programme, which gives viewers an opportunity to express their opinions about programmes of all kinds.

## Activities

James Kirkup has published several volumes of poetry and has contributed poems to many anthologies for children. He now lives in Japan. (For further details see page 164.)

Fritz Spiegl's *The Games All About Clichés, Innit?* appeared in *The Independent* on September 1st 1988.

## Points of view

### Group work

1 Choose someone to act as presenter and prepare a simulated presentation of the letters with other members of the group reading the various letters. Discuss together how the letters should be read and what impression of the writer you want to give, then rehearse your reading, before presenting it to the rest of the class.

2 Discuss the letters about the amount of sports coverage on TV. Which of the three letters do you think argues the person's case most effectively?

3 Talk about sports commentators. Do you find their comments irksome or informative? Which of the letters in this section do you think puts across the writer's viewpoint most clearly and effectively? (Note: your decision should be based on how well the writer expresses herself/himself, not on how much you agree/disagree with the writer's opinions!)

4 What other issues about sports coverage on TV do you have strong views about, e.g. the timing of sports programmes; sports quiz programmes; the length of time devoted to the build up to an event, such as a cup final; anything else? Share your views in a group discussion about sports coverge on TV.

5 Decide on an appropriate motion and organize a formal debate about sports coverage on TV.

### Written assignments

1 Working in a group, each write at least one letter expressing your views about sport on TV, then choose a presenter, rehearse and present a selection of your letters about sports coverage on TV.

2 Write a discursive essay stating your views about sport on TV.

Activities

## The Dartist

Pair work

1 What impression do you get of the dartist in Alan Bold's poem? What do you think the writer's attitude is towards him?
2 Talk about sports which, like darts, have become more popular as a result of TV coverage, e.g. snooker, American football, bowls, sumo wrestling. Are some sports more suitable than others for showing on TV? Discuss which sports you think make good television.

## Sumo Wrestlers

Group work

Work through the poem section by section discussing what each says, how it is said and what your response to that section is. Which section is the most effective? Say why.

## The Game's All About Clichés, Innit?

Pair work

1 Video-tape or tape-record an extract of sports commentary. Listen to it carefully and pick out all the clichés that the commentator uses.
2 Compile a file of reports on events in one particular sport, e.g. football, tennis, athletics, from a range of different newspapers. Compare the reports. Do journalists from different newspapers write in different styles about the same sport? Do some journalists use more clichés than others? Share your findings in a class discussion. Then, do one of the written assignments about clichés suggested below.
3 Most sports have their own technical language or jargon, consisting of specialist terms used in connection with that particular sport. For example, cricketers refer to square leg, no-balls and extras; rugby players to tries and conversions; tennis-players to deuce and tie-breaks, etc. Work with a partner and compile a glossary of specialist terms that are used in one particular sport. Then, write a paragraph describing an imaginary incident in your chosen sport, in which you use as many jargon words as possible. Try re-writing the same paragraph omitting all the specialist terms and using only language that someone

## Activities

unfamiliar with the sport would understand. Compare the two versions and talk about why people use jargon when talking or writing about sports.

### Written assignments

1  Write a parody of a sports commentary using as many clichés as possible. Make the events the commentator is describing as ludicrous and far-fetched as you wish.

2  Use Fritz Spiegl's article as a model and prepare a similar article about the clichés used by people giving commentaries on a sport other than football.

## *Just for Fun*

### Background notes

Max Boyce was born in the Welsh mining village of Glynneath. He left school at fifteen and worked in the local colliery before embarking on a career as an entertainer. *Playing for Wales* comes from a collection of his poems, stories and songs, *I was there*!

Ian McDonald's *The Village Cricket Match* is an adaptation of a story from *The Humming-bird Tree*.

Geraldine Kaye lives in Bristol and is a well-known writer of books for young people. Her novels include *A Breath of Fresh Air* and *Comfort Herself*.

### Playing for Wales

#### Group work

1  As you read Max Boyce's account of his childhood memories, did it remind you of games that you have played in the street or in the park? Share any memories of these games and of particular incidents that you recall vividly, such as accidents or quarrels.

2  Talk about how Max Boyce embroiders his memories in order to create a humorous effect. Pick out any details which you think he has deliberately exaggerated.

Activities

3  Discuss the conversational style in which Max Boyce writes, as if he is actually speaking to the reader. Pick out features of his writing that are common features of spoken language.

### Written assignment

Write about your memories of games you have played on the rec or in the playground, in the way that Max Boyce writes about his memories. Use a conversational style and, if appropriate, exaggerate in order to make your account more humorous.

## The Village Cricket Match

### Group work

1  The narrator says in the second paragraph that the game was 'hilariously, intensely and fiercely contested.' What evidence is there in his account of the match to support that statement?
2  Discuss the incident that occurred when Kaiser struck the ball and it accidentally hit his mother's cow. Who do you sympathize with most – Kaiser, his mother or his father? Say why. Did it remind you any incidents you have been involved in because you kicked, threw or struck a ball which hit somebody or something? Share your memories of such incidents.

### Written assignments

1  Have you ever attended a very bizarre sports event or seen anything very unusual happen as a spectator? Use your memory as the starting point for a story.
2  Compare Ian McDonald's story with Michael Parkinson's story *Clakker May*. What similarities are there in the way the writers tell their stories?

## The Day I Ran for England

### Group work

1  As you read Geraldine Kaye's account of her athletic career, did it remind you of any moments of sporting failure or success in your own life? Share your memories in a group discussion.

### Activities

2  Talk about the incidents Geraldine Kaye describes and discuss her attitudes towards each of them. Talk about how she satirizes herself and her sporting achievements.

### Written assignment

Pick out two or three memories of incidents that sum up your sporting life and write about them in the way that Geraldine Kaye writes about her sporting career.

# Extended Activities

## Essays

1 Choose one story, one autobiographical piece, one poem and one non-fiction piece from this selection. Explain why you think they are the most interesting examples to choose and say what is special or distinctive about each piece. Think about such things as: ideas, subject, style and technique of the writing.
2 Choose two short stories from the selection and compare them, focusing on the style, technique and the ideas they convey.

## A playscript

Choose one of the stories which you think would make a good television or radio play and write a script for it. Preface your script with a note, explaining why you chose this particular story.

## An extended essay

Choose one of the topics listed below and start by studying the appropriate pieces in this anthology;
**Women and sport**   See *Unfair, The Ref's a Woman, Miss Willis P.E., A Life in the Day of Joanne Conway, Glove me Tender.*
**Sport and the media**   See the section *Sport on TV* and Gareth Owen's poem *The Commentator.*
**Violence and sport**   See *I Didn't Do Nothing* and the section *But Is It Sport?*
**Sport and politics**   See *Moral Rules to Every Game.*
**Sport in schools**   See the section *Sports in School*. Investigate the topic further by watching any relevant TV programmes and collecting magazines and newspaper articles that are related to it. Then, write an essay exploring the issues connected to that particular topic. Before you begin, brainstorm with your group the ideas that you are going to include and discuss them first with a partner, then with your teacher.

Extended Activities

## A Magazine Article

Work in a group and each produce an item for a sports magazine. Decide whether yours is going to be a specialist magazine focusing on one particular sport or a general magazine with items on many sports. Discuss who it is aimed at – is it aimed exclusively at young people or is it for people of all ages?

Study copies of magazines that are available in the library or that you can bring in and decide what sort of items you would want to include in your magazine. Some things that you might include are: reports and accounts of games that you have seen or played in; articles about teams, clubs and individuals; previews of important occasions; articles giving hints on how to improve your skills; articles on sports equipment, comparing different products and saying where they can be bought; articles on controversial sporting issues.

When you have decided which sort of article you are going to write, draw up an outline of it. Then discuss your outlines together before beginning to draft your articles.

## Oral assignment

Work in a group and produce a short radio programme (either 5 or 10 minutes) entitled *Sporting Matters*. Discuss the type of items you could include, such as reports, interviews, studio discussions, extracts from commentaries, book reviews, previews and listeners' letters. Research and draft the various items you plan to include. Choose someone to act as presenter, discuss a running order and produce a linking script. Then, tape-record your programme.

# Wider Reading

## Assignments

Choose one of the books from the booklist given below, read it and then write a review of it. When you are writing a review of a book it can be helpful to focus on a passage that you found particularly interesting or dull, sad or funny, or significant for some other reason. Focusing on a passage can often help you to think of a way to start your review. When you are reviewing a book with a sporting background, here are some questions to ask while you are drafting your review:
1   What impression of the central character do you get? How well does the author explain the part that sport plays in the person's life?
2   Think about the other characters. How well are they described? Did you find it easy to form a picture of them? Was their relationship with the main character clearly described?
3   How successfully does the author describe any training sessions and sports events? Are the descriptions authentic? Do they manage to capture the atmosphere of the sessions/events?
4   Think about the ending of the story. Did you find it satisfying? Could the book have ended in any other way?
5   How well do the events of the story fit together? Did you find the plot plausible or far-fetched? What do you see as being the strengths and weaknesses of the book's plot?
6   Think about how the story is written. Is it presented through the eyes of one particular character? How does the viewpont from which it is written affect the story? Would the story have worked any better if it had been presented from a different viewpoint?
7   How would you sum up your response to the book? What sort of person do you think would enjoy reading it? Would you recommend it?

Peter Carter, *Bury the Dead,* Oxford, 1986; Fontana Lions, 1988
Aidan Chambers ed., *A Sporting Chance*, Bodley Head, 1985
Tony Drake, *Playing it Right*, Puffin, 1981
Eamon Dunphy, *Only a game*, Kestrel, 1976
Bill Forsyth, *Gregory's Girl*
Brian Glanville, *Goalkeepers are Crazy*, Longman, 1977
Barry Hines, *The Blinder*, Penguin, 1969

## Wider Reading

| | |
|---|---|
| Clive Jermain, | *The Best Years of Your Life* |
| | *A Special Occasion* Longman |
| Tim Kennemore | *The Fortunate Few* Penguin *Plus* 1983 |
| Julius Lester, | *Basketball Game* Heinemann Educational 1989 |
| Anthony Masters, | *Murphy and Co* Penguin *Plus* |
| | *The Return of Murphy's Mob* Penguin *Plus* |
| *Michael Saunders,* | *Murphy's Mob* Penguin *Plus* |
| *Vernon Scannell,* | *The Big Time*, Longman, 1969 |
| David Storey, | *This Sporting Life*, Longman, 1960 |
| Peter Terson, | *Zigger Zagger*, Penguin, 1970 |
| Mark Wheeler and | |
| Alison Leake ed., | *Race to be Seen*, Longman, 1986 |
| Ian Woodward ed., | *Football Stories*, Carousel, 1984 |